Englisch

ABSCHLUSS-
PRÜFUNGS-
TRAINER

Mittlerer Schulabschluss
Nordrhein-Westfalen

 Deine Online-Angebote findest du hier:

1. Melde dich auf scook.de an.
2. Gib den unten stehenden Zugangscode in die Box ein.
3. Hab viel Spaß mit den Online-Angeboten.

Dein Zugangscode auf
www.scook.de

Die Online-Angebote können dort
nach Bestätigung der AGB und
Lizenzbedingungen genutzt werden.

qctg2-s26q7

Cornelsen

Abschlussprüfungstrainer Englisch
Mittlerer Schulabschluss | Nordrhein-Westfalen

Erarbeitet von:
Gwen Berwick, York
Sydney Thorne, York

In Zusammenarbeit mit der Englischredaktion: Klaus Unger (Projektleitung); Cornelia Frisse (verantwortliche Redakteurin); Nicola Regner

Beratende Mitwirkung: Peer Brändel, Gütersloh

Illustrationen: Karen Donnelly, Brighton

Layout-Konzept: Klein&Halm Grafikdesign, Berlin

Umschlaggestaltung: Agentur Rosendahl, Berlin

Layout und technische Umsetzung: Klein&Halm Grafikdesign, Berlin

www.cornelsen.de

Soweit in diesem Lehrwerk Personen fotografisch abgebildet sind und ihnen von der Redaktion fiktive Namen, Berufe, Dialoge und Ähnliches zugeordnet oder diese Personen in bestimmte Kontexte gesetzt werden, dienen diese Zuordnungen und Darstellungen ausschließlich der Veranschaulichung und dem besseren Verständnis des Inhalts.

1. Auflage, 1. Druck 2017

Druck: Firmengruppe APPL, aprinta Druck, Wemding

ISBN 978-3-06-034856-5

PEFC zertifiziert
Dieses Produkt stammt aus nachhaltig
bewirtschafteten Wäldern und kontrollierten
Quellen.
www.pefc.de
PEFC/04-32-0928

Inhaltsverzeichnis

Vorwort

Training Section

Hörverstehen – *Listening*

Leseverstehen – *Reading*

Wortschatz – *Vocabulary*

Schreiben – *Writing*

Musterprüfungen

Lösungen (als Einleger in der Mitte des Heftes)

Was erwartet dich in der Prüfung?

Liebe Schülerin, lieber Schüler,

bald ist es für dich so weit und du legst die zentrale Prüfung im Fach Englisch ab. Damit du weißt, was auf dich zukommt, wollen wir dir genau erklären, was dich in der Prüfung erwartet und wie du dich optimal vorbereiten kannst.

Die zentrale Prüfung Englisch im Überblick

Die zentrale Prüfung besteht aus zwei Teilen und dauert insgesamt 120 Minuten. Zusätzlich erhältst du zehn Minuten Bonuszeit, die du frei zur Orientierung oder zum Überprüfen deiner Lösungen einsetzen kannst.

	Kompetenz	Ausgangstexte und Aufgaben	Zeit	Punkte

Erster Prüfungsteil	Hörverstehen	• zwei Hörtexte
		• verschiedene Aufgabenformate:
		  – Auswahlaufgaben *(Multiple choice)*
		  – Zuordnungsaufgaben *(Matching)*
		  – Einsetzaufgaben *(Fill in the gap)*
		  – etc.
			40 Minuten	18 Punkte

	Leseverstehen	• ein Lesetext
		• verschiedene Aufgabenformate:
		  – Auswahlaufgaben *(Multiple choice)*
		  – Richtig/Falsch-Aufgaben *(True/False)*
		  – Kurzantwort-Aufgaben
		  – etc.
				18 Punkte

Zweiter Prüfungsteil	Wortschatz	• ein Lesetext bzw. einzelne Sätze
		• verschiedene Aufgabenformate:
		  – Auswahlaufgaben *(Multiple choice)*
		  – Zuordnungsaufgaben *(Matching)*
		  – Einsetzaufgaben *(Fill in the gap)*
		  – etc.
			80 Minuten	12 Punkte

	Schreiben	• ein Lesetext
		• verschiedene Aufgabenformate:
		  – Textverständnis
		  – Interpretation
		  – argumentatives Schreiben
		  – kreatives Schreiben
				72 Punkte

			120 Minuten + 10 Minuten Bonuszeit	120 Punkte

Themen, Texte und Hilfsmittel in der Prüfung

In der Prüfung wird nicht dein Wissen über ein Thema oder ein Land abgefragt. Das Themenfeld dient nur als kultureller und sprachlicher Rahmen für den Test. Die Texte in der Prüfung beziehen sich auf die wichtigsten englischsprachigen Länder wie Großbritannien, die USA, Australien, Kanada, Neuseeland, Südafrika, Indien, Pakistan, Jamaika etc. Alle Textsorten (Zeitungsartikel, Brief, Dialog, Radio-Interview, Präsentation, Cartoon etc.), denen du in der Prüfung begegnest, werden dir aus deinem Englischunterricht vertraut sein.

Übrigens: Während der Prüfung sind keine Hilfsmittel erlaubt, auch **keine Wörterbücher**. In diesem Heft findest du daher auch Übungen und Tipps, die dir helfen, unbekannte Wörter und Aussagen zu entschlüsseln. Mach dir aber gleichzeitig bewusst, dass du nicht jedes einzelne Wort kennen musst, um einen Text in seinen wichtigsten Aussagen zu verstehen.

Erster Prüfungsteil: Hör- und Leseverstehen

Der **erste Teil des Tests** besteht aus zwei Hörtexten und einem Lesetext. Hörtexte wirst du immer zweimal hören. Zwischenfragen an die Lehrkraft sind nicht erlaubt.

Es gibt unterschiedliche Aufgabenformate, die dir alle aus dem Englischunterricht bekannt sind:

- **Auswahlaufgaben** *(Multiple choice)*: Hier werden dir drei bis vier mögliche Lösungen angeboten und du musst die richtige heraussuchen, indem du das richtige Kästchen ankreuzt.
- **Richtig/Falsch-Aufgaben** *(True/False)*: Bei derartigen Aufgaben musst du entscheiden, ob die vorgegebene Aussage über den Text wahr oder falsch ist. Oft (meist beim Leseverstehen) musst du auch noch die passende Textstelle aus dem Text heraussuchen und zitieren, um deine Entscheidung zu begründen.
- **Zuordnungsaufgaben** *(Matching)*: Bei diesen Aufgaben musst du z. B. Textstellen einer Auswahl an Bildern, Aussagen oder Personen zuordnen.
- **Einsetzaufgaben** *(Fill in the gap)*: Bei diesen Aufgaben musst du in deinen eigenen Worten Sätze vervollständigen oder Wörter einsetzen.
- **Kurzantwort-Aufgaben** *(Giving short answers)*: Hier beantwortest du in deinen eigenen Worten Fragen oder gibst für bestimmte Aussagen Beispiele aus dem Text.
- **Sequenzierungsaufgaben** *(Put in the right order)*: Bei derartigen Aufgaben bringst du Bilder, Aussagen, Themen etc. in die richtige Reihenfolge.

Zweiter Prüfungsteil: Wortschatz und Schreiben

Der **zweite Teil des Tests** besteht ebenfalls aus zwei Teilen:

Zunächst werden deine **Wortschatzkenntnisse** abgeprüft. Dies geschieht durch folgende Aufgabentypen:
- **Einsetzaufgaben** *(Fill in the gap)*: Bei diesem sehr häufig eingesetzten Aufgabenformat setzt du in einen Text passende Wörter oder Begriffe ein.
- **Auswahlaufgaben** *(Multiple choice)*: Oft erhältst du dafür eine Auswahl an Begriffen und musst dich für den passendsten entscheiden.
- Auch können dir **Zuordnungsaufgaben** *(Matching)* begegnen, bei denen du z. B. Synonyme, Gegensätze oder Umschreibungen zuordnen musst.
- Bei **Ergänzungsaufgaben** musst du z. B. Wörter zu einem vorgegebenen Thema ergänzen.

Es schließt sich ein Lesetext an, der bestimmte Probleme und Fragen aufwirft, zu denen du **Schreibaufgaben** bearbeiten sollst:
- Die ersten beiden Aufgaben beziehen sich direkt auf den Inhalt dieses Textes, kombinieren also Leseverstehen und Schreiben:
  - Bei **Aufgabe 1** wird abgeprüft, ob du bestimmte Aspekte des Textes verstanden hast und wiedergeben kannst. Diese Aufgaben beginnen meist mit der Aufforderung *Describe* …
  - Bei **Aufgabe 2** sollst du zeigen, dass du grundlegende Aspekte des Textes auch interpretieren kannst. Diese Aufgaben beginnen meist mit der Aufforderung *Explain* …
  Du musst beide Aufgaben bearbeiten.

- Die dritte Aufgabe geht über den Lesetext hinaus, hier schreibst du selbst einen längeren Text. Du erhältst **zwei Alternativen** (a und b) zur Auswahl:
  - **a) argumentatives Schreiben:** Du schreibst einen Kommentar *(comment)* zu einer Aussage, die thematisch mit dem Lesetext verbunden ist. Hier diskutierst du die *pros* und *cons*, wägst ab, findest Beispiele für deine Argumentation und kommst zu einem begründeten Ergebnis.

    oder

  - **b) kreatives Schreiben:** Hier gibt es vielfältige Aufgaben, z. B. musst du eine Fortsetzung oder ein alternatives Ende zum Lesetext schreiben, die Perspektive wechseln, einen Dialog zwischen den Personen, die im Lesetext vorkommen, verfassen, einen Brief, eine E-Mail oder einen Tagebucheintrag schreiben, in Form eines Zeitungsartikels über die Inhalte des Ausgangstextes berichten etc.

Wie arbeitest du mit diesem Heft?

In diesem Heft lernst du durch gezielte Übungen, wie du die Aufgaben zu allen Prüfungsteilen bearbeiten kannst. Darüber hinaus bekommst du konkrete Prüfungsbeispiele. Das Heft ist deshalb wie folgt aufgebaut:

Das **erste Kapitel**, die *Training Section*, gliedert sich in die vier Kompetenzbereiche, die in der zentralen Prüfung abgeprüft werden: **Hörverstehen**, **Leseverstehen**, **Wortschatz** und **Schreiben**.

Die *Training Section* enthält:

Tipp

Blau umrandete Felder markieren Tipps, die dir bei den Aufgaben helfen.

- Hinweise zum Ablauf und zur Bewertung jedes einzelnen Kompetenzbereichs
- Beispiele und Tipps für alle Aufgabenformate, die in der Prüfung vorkommen können, also *Multiple choice*, *True/False* etc.
- zahlreiche Strategien zum Umgang mit typischen Schwierigkeiten, wie z. B. Verständnisproblemen
- vielfältige Aufgaben zum Üben deines Hör- und Leseverständnisses sowie deiner Wortschatzkenntnisse *(Now you)*.

Es empfiehlt sich, die *Training Section* als erstes durchzuarbeiten, und zwar Kompetenzbereich für Kompetenzbereich. So verschaffst du dir einen Überblick darüber, was du schon gut kannst, wo du noch üben solltest und welche Strategien dir dabei helfen.

Das **zweite Kapitel** bietet dir drei komplette **Musterprüfungen**, die jeweils alle vier Kompetenzbereiche (Hörverstehen, Leseverstehen, Wortschatz, Schreiben) enthalten. Sie sind den Prüfungen der letzten Jahre nachempfunden. Du lernst dadurch Schritt für Schritt die gesamte Prüfungssituation und den Aufbau einer Prüfung kennen.

Wenn du feststellst, dass du mit einem Kompetenzbereich oder einem Aufgabenformat noch Schwierigkeiten hast, gehe zurück in die *Training Section* und wiederhole gezielt die entsprechenden Übungen und Strategien oder nutze die Online-Übungen zu Grammatik und Wortschatz auf www.scook.de.

Die **Tonaufnahmen und Hörtexte** für die *Training Section* und die Musterprüfungen findest du ebenfalls online unter www.scook.de. Das Kopfhörer-Symbol mit Track-Nummer im Heft zeigt dir an, welchen Hörtext du für die Aufgabe anhören musst.

Mit dem **Lösungsteil** in der Mitte des Heftes kannst du deine Ergebnisse überprüfen und – wenn nötig – verbessern. Dort findest du auch eine Tabelle zur Benotung.

Nützliche Tipps zur Prüfungsvorbereitung erhältst du auf S. 69.

Nun kannst du zuversichtlich sein, dass du weißt, was in der zentralen Prüfung auf dich zukommt, und dass du die unterschiedlichen Aufgabenstellungen geübt hast und kennst.

> Zusätzlich kannst du dein Grundwissen in den Bereichen Grammatik und Wortschatz mithilfe von Online-Übungen wiederholen und vertiefen. Nutze dazu den Zugangscode auf Seite 1 (www.scook.de).
>
> Ebenfalls online findest du die Tonaufnahmen zu den Höraufgaben als MP3-Downloads, die Hörtexte sowie die Originalprüfungen früherer Jahre mit Lösungen. Nutze dazu ebenfalls den Code von Seite 1.

Viel Spaß beim Training mit diesem Heft und viel Erfolg bei der Prüfung!

ABSCHLUSS-PRÜFUNGS-TRAINER

Nordrhein-Westfalen

Training Section

Hörverstehen – *Listening*

1. Ablauf und Bewertung der Prüfung

Erster Prüfungsteil

Im **ersten Prüfungsteil** geht es um **Hörverstehen und Leseverstehen**. Dafür hast du insgesamt 40 Minuten Zeit. Zusätzlich erhältst du zehn Minuten Bonuszeit, die du verwenden kannst, wie du willst – du kannst diese Zeit z. B. nutzen, um dir einen Überblick über die Aufgaben zu verschaffen oder um deine Lösungen nochmals zu überprüfen. Du kannst dir die Bonuszeit aber auch für den zweiten Prüfungsteil aufheben. In diesen maximal 50 (40 + 10) Minuten musst du zwei Hörtexte und einen Lesetext bearbeiten. Wenn du mit dem ersten Prüfungsteil (Hörverstehen und Leseverstehen) früher fertig bist, hast du entsprechend mehr Zeit für den zweiten Prüfungsteil (Wortschatz und Schreiben).

Ablauf beim Hörverstehen

Beim **Hörverstehen** hast du zunächst 90 Sekunden Zeit, um die Aufgaben zu lesen. Dann hörst du den Hörtext zum ersten Mal. Du bearbeitest die Aufgaben und hörst abschließend den Hörtext noch ein zweites Mal. Dies ist das Vorgehen bei beiden Hörtexten der Zentralprüfung.

Bewertung beim Hörverstehen

Ein Wörterbuch ist beim Hörverstehen nicht erlaubt. Du brauchst aber keine Angst vor Grammatik- oder Rechtschreibfehlern in deinen Antworten zu haben. Solange man versteht, was du geschrieben hast, gehen sie in diesem Prüfungsteil nicht in die Bewertung ein. Das Hörverstehen macht 15 % deiner Gesamtnote aus.

2. Typische Aufgabenformate in NRW

In diesem Kapitel lernst du anhand eines Radio-Interviews über die kanadische Stadt Calgary die typischen Aufgabenformate kennen, die dich bei der Zentralprüfung im Bereich Hörverstehen erwarten. Die Tipp-Kästen enthalten nützliche Strategien, wie du mit häufigen Schwierigkeiten umgehen kannst.

Calgary's skyways

You are going to hear a radio interview about the skyway network in Calgary, a city in western Canada.

Auswahlaufgaben *(Multiple choice)*

> - *First read the task.*
> - *Then listen to the first part of the interview.*
> - *While you are listening, tick the correct box.*
> - *At the end you will hear the interview again.*

An underground city ...

a) ☐ is a famous tourist site in Calgary.

b) ☐ can be very cold.

c) ☐ allows people to avoid the cold weather.

Tipp

Bei *Multiple choice*-Aufgaben werden einzelne Wörter aus dem Hörtext häufig ersetzt durch:

Synonyme:
climate im Hörtext   =   *weather* in Antwort c)

Gegensätze:
exposed to (the climate) ≠ *avoid (the weather)*
im Hörtext   in Antwort c)
(dem Klima) ausgesetzt   (das Wetter) vermeiden

Verneinte Gegensätze:
Manchmal wird ein Gegensatz durch Wörter wie *not* oder *without* aber auch wieder in sein Gegenteil gekehrt. Das wirkt dann wie ein Synonym – also durch unterschiedliche Formulierungen wird Ähnliches ausgesagt. So auch hier:

without being exposed   =   *avoid (the weather)*
(to the climate)
<u>ohne</u> (dem Klima) ausgesetzt zu sein   (das Wetter) vermeiden

Das spricht hier dafür, dass Antwort c) richtig ist.

Zuordnungsaufgaben *(Matching)*

- *First read the task.*
- *Then listen to the second part of the interview and match the place names (1–5) with the pictures (A–F). You won't need one picture.*
- *At the end you will hear the interview again.*

Overhead pedestrian passage in Calgary

Tipp

- Musst du Bilder zuordnen, so überlege, wie das Dargestellte auf Englisch heißen könnte. Bild **B** zeigt hier z. B. ein Freiluft-Kino. Achte im Hörtext also auf Begriffe wie *movie, watch, cinema, open air* oder *theatre*.
- Achtung! Die Ortsnamen können im Hörtext in einer anderen Reihenfolge vorkommen.

1 Burlington: _____

2 Stoney Creek: _____

3 Kissimmee: _____

4 Jacksonville: _____

5 Jasper National Park: _____

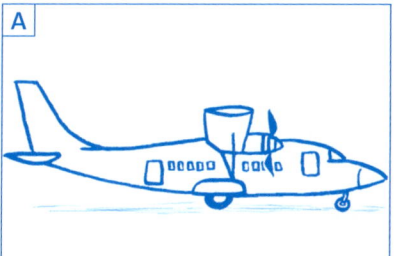

Einsetzaufgaben *(Fill in the gap)*

- *First read the tasks (1–2).*
- *Then listen to the third part of the interview.*
- *While you are listening, fill in the information.*
- *At the end you will hear the interview again.*

1 Calgary has a system of _____

passageways 15 feet up in the air.

Tipp

Denke an den Sinn der fehlenden Wörter. Die *passageways* sind in der Luft, **über deinem Kopf** …

2 There are passageways between buildings all

over _____ Calgary.

Kurzantwort-Aufgaben *(Giving short answers)*

> • *First read the tasks (1–2).*
> • *Then listen to the fourth part of the interview and answer the questions.*
> • *At the end you will hear the interview again.*

1 What are **two** advantages for pedestrians?

a) _____

b) _____

2 Why do some people criticize the skyways?

_____

> **Tipp**
> • Bei diesem Aufgabentyp sollst du die Antworten in deinen eigenen Worten geben. Du brauchst nicht Wort für Wort aus dem Hörtext zu zitieren.
> • Fragen mit zwei Teilen – a) und b) – sind zwei Punkte wert. Gib also zwei verschiedene Antworten.

Richtig/Falsch-Aufgaben *(True/False)*

> • *First read the task.*
> • *Then listen to the fifth part of the interview and tick the correct box.*
> • *At the end you will hear the interview again.*

1 Over 22,000 people use the busiest bridge every weekend.

This statement is ... ☐ true ☐ false

2 Harold Hanen was born in Calgary.

This statement is ... ☐ true ☐ false

3 He did some of his studies abroad.

This statement is ... ☐ true ☐ false

> **Tipp**
> • Vorsicht in Sätzen mit Zahlen: Achte nicht nur auf die Zahl, sondern auch auf den Rest des Satzes, z. B. *every weekend* in **Satz 1**.
> • Achte auch auf **Synonyme**, z. B. *a native of* im Hörtext = *born in* in **Satz 2**.

3. Umgang mit Verständnisproblemen

Die Hörtexte in der Zentralprüfung enthalten manchmal Wörter, die du vielleicht nicht kennst oder die du auch beim ersten oder zweiten Hören nicht verstehst. Das ist ganz normal. Also keine Panik – es gibt Strategien, die dir helfen, die wesentlichen Inhalte trotzdem zu erfassen und die Aufgabe zu lösen. In diesem Kapitel werden anhand eines Werbefilms über die Niagarafälle die wichtigsten Strategien vorgestellt.

The Niagara Falls

The following text is the audio track of a publicity film about the Niagara Falls.

> • *First read the tasks (1–5).*
> • *Then listen to the programme. You can read the text while you listen.*
> • *Do tasks 1–5: tick the correct box or fill in the information.*
> • *At the end you will hear the text again (task 6).*

Tipp

Die Tonaufnahme (Track 6) enthält Störgeräusche, die einige Textstellen unverständlich machen. Im Hörtext sind diese Stellen durch Schwärzungen kenntlich gemacht. Dieses Vorgehen soll dir verdeutlichen, dass du einige der Aufgaben 1–5 trotz der fehlenden Textstellen lösen kannst. Bei anderen Aufgaben kannst du mithilfe der Tipps zumindest Vermutungen anstellen.

Beim zweiten Hören (Track 7) in Aufgabe 6 hörst du den Text ohne Störgeräusche. Nun kannst du überprüfen, ob deine Vermutungen richtig waren.

Welcome to the Niagara Falls! These astonishing natural waterfalls are on the border between the USA and Canada. They consist of three waterfalls. The two smaller ones are in the USA. But these amazing falls, called the Horseshoe Falls, are the biggest and they're ▮▮▮ in Canada. The Niagara Falls are located near important urban centres. It only takes half an hour by car to get to Buffalo.

These tourists have just landed at Buffalo International Airport and they're on their way to see the famous falls. In fact, about 30 million people visit the Niagara Falls each year! This group is going on the very popular *Maid of the Mist* tour – a boat tour to the bottom of the waterfalls. The air here is full of ▮▮▮▮▮ ▮▮▮▮▮ – that's why everyone here is wearing ▮▮▮▮▮. But don't be fooled – most of them are going to get wet anyway. Oh! Here comes the next shower!

Accessing the falls is easy. That's great because it means that thousands of people can come and see the fantastic sight. But it also means that the falls have to be well protected and taken care of. In fact, these falls on the American side are actually part of ▮▮▮▮ ▮▮▮ state park. It was designed by the same man who laid out this well-known park. Do you recognize it? It's Central Park in New York City. Luckily state parks don't charge entrance – so you don't have to pay to see the falls. Tourists can stand right next to the top of the Horseshoe Falls and watch the water spilling over. Isn't it amazing?

Sometimes people have gone over the falls. Some have even done it by choice. This is Annie Taylor – she was the first person to ride over the Niagara Falls, way back in 1901, on her 63rd birthday. After her husband and son had died, Annie was facing poverty and decided to go over the falls ▮▮▮▮▮. And guess what she used to cross the falls: this thing. That's right – a wooden barrel. The sort of barrel that was used to store wine or beer. Crazy, isn't it? She put cushions and a mattress inside and asked some friends to push the barrel in the right direction at the top – and other friends to open it when she got to the bottom of the falls. And she did: she went over the top of the falls, the barrel fell, and when her friends opened it, she was alive. But although Annie (amazingly!) came out with no broken bones, she ▮▮▮▮▮: it was bleeding. After her crazy experiment, Annie warned other people against doing the same thing. We'll take your advice, Annie.

1 The Horseshoe Falls …

a) ☐ are smaller than the American falls.

b) ☐ are fully in Canada.

c) ☐ are for the most part in Canada.

Tipp

Wenn du nicht gleich auf die richtige Antwort kommst, wende das Ausschlussverfahren an:
- Markiere die Stelle im ersten Absatz, die Antwort a) ausschließt.
- Zwischen b) und c) kannst du dich noch nicht entscheiden: Im Hörtext könnte es nämlich heißen **only** in Canada, **mainly** in Canada, **partly** in Canada oder **fully** in Canada.

Also wirst du nochmals hören müssen. Aber jetzt kannst du gezielt zwischen zwei möglichen Antworten entscheiden – das ist leichter als zwischen drei.

2 The people on the boat tours need protection. Give **one** example of how they protect themselves.

Tipp

Hier kannst du dir helfen, indem du Vermutungen anstellst:
- Die Touristen sind laut Hörtext *wet* (= nass).
- Wie kann man sich gegen Nässe schützen? Zu erwarten sind also Wörter wie *raincoat*, *umbrella*, *waterproof* etc.

Achte beim zweiten Zuhören besonders gut auf diese Stelle. Mit dieser Vorbereitung wirst du sie bestimmt besser verstehen.

3 The land on the American side of the falls ...

  a) ☐ can only be reached if you pay.

  b) ☐ was the first state park in the USA.

  c) ☐ looks like Central Park in New York City.

> **Tipp**
>
> Wende das Ausschlussverfahren an!
> Lösung c) kannst du sogar, wenn du fast nichts verstanden hast, mit dem gesunden Menschenverstand ausschließen. Warum?
>
> Lösung a) kannst du ebenfalls ausschließen, wenn du die relevante Stelle im Text verstanden hast. Markiere diese Stelle.

4 Annie Taylor went over the falls in a barrel in

  order to _____ .

> **Tipp**
>
> Was weißt du über Annie Taylor? Kannst du daraus schließen, zu welchem Zweck sie so etwas Gefährliches gemacht hat?

5 When Annie Taylor's friends opened the barrel, they found that she was ...

  a) ☐ dead.

  b) ☐ injured.

  c) ☐ unhurt.

> **Tipp**
>
> • Markiere das Wort im Hörtext, mit dem du Lösung a) ausschließen kannst.
> • Das Wort *although* (= obwohl) im Text leitet einen Gegensatz ein: Obwohl sie nichts gebrochen hatte, war sie _____ .
> Dank dieses Wortes kannst du also beim zweiten Hören zwischen Lösung b) und Lösung c) wählen. Siehst du wie?

🎧
7
> • *Now read tasks 6 and 7.*
> • *Then listen to the programme again. This time it's complete.*
> • *Do task 6 while you are listening.*
> • *Then do task 7.*

6 Listen to the complete programme. Note the exact words in the recording.

  a) ... the Horseshoe Falls are the biggest and they're _____ in Canada.

  b) ... everyone here is wearing _____ .

  c) ... these falls on the American side are actually part of _____ state park.

  d) Annie (...) decided to go over the falls to _____ .

  e) But although Annie (amazingly!) came out with no broken bones, she _____

    _____ – it was bleeding.

7 Now use your information from task **6** to check your answers to tasks **1–5**.

4. Hörverstehen – *Now you*

In diesem Kapitel kannst du die Strategien, die du auf den letzten Seiten kennen gelernt hast, bei ausgewählten Aufgaben zum Hörverstehen gezielt üben. Grundlage dafür sind ein Dialog über ein Radrennen in Yorkshire sowie ein Radio-Interview über die jamaikanische Reggae-Legende Bob Marley.

The Tour de Yorkshire

Sarah from Ireland and Mo from Yorkshire are talking about a cycling race in Yorkshire. You will hear their telephone conversation.

Auswahlaufgaben *(Multiple choice)*

> • *First read the tasks (1–5).*
> • *Then listen to the dialogue.*
> • *While you are listening, tick the correct box.*
> • *At the end you will hear the dialogue again.*
> • *Now read the tasks. You have 90 seconds to do this.*

> • *Now listen to the dialogue and do the tasks.*

Yellow bicycle on the city walls of York, 2014

1 In 2014 the Tour de France cycling race …

   a) ☐ began in France and came to Yorkshire.

   b) ☐ went through other countries and then came to Yorkshire.

   c) ☐ began in Yorkshire.

2 During the stages of the race in Yorkshire …

   a) ☐ cycling fans rode yellow bicycles on the sides of the roads used by the race.

   b) ☐ people bought lots of yellow bicycles.

   c) ☐ there were old yellow bicycles on the sides of the roads used by the race.

3 The organizers of the Tour de France …

   a) ☐ planned for large crowds.

   b) ☐ didn't expect the enthusiastic reaction from people in Yorkshire.

   c) ☐ hoped that many people would join the cyclists.

4 The Tour de France …

   a) ☐ was in Yorkshire for 21 days.

   b) ☐ left people in Yorkshire wanting to see more cycling races.

   c) ☐ went from Yorkshire directly on to France.

5 The Tour de Yorkshire cycling race …

   a) ☐ includes hills that are difficult even for experienced cyclists.

   b) ☐ uses wide roads to allow for big groups of cyclists to pass through.

   c) ☐ has become a very popular off-road race.

Bob Marley

Radio presenter Joshua Needham is talking to Reggae expert Gwen Devlin about the Jamaican singer-songwriter Bob Marley.

Gemischte Aufgabenformate (Mixed tasks)

> • First read the tasks (1–8).
> • Then listen to the interview.
> • While you are listening, tick the correct box, match the sentence halves, say if the statements are true or false or answer the questions.
> • At the end you will hear the interview again.
> • Now read the tasks. You have 90 seconds to do this.

> • Now listen to the interview and do the tasks.

Bob Marley (1945–1981)

1 Match the people (1–3) with the sentence halves (A–E). Each person can match with one or more sentence halves.

1 Bob Marley …	**A** used to live in Sussex, England.
2 Bob Marley's father …	**B** lived in Nine Miles for many years.
3 Bob Marley's mother …	**C** was born in February 1945.
	D was 18 when Bob was born.
	E died of a heart attack.

2 Kingston was important in Bob Marley's musical life.

This statement is … ☐ true ☐ false … because Gwen says …

_____

3 Bob Marley's early song *Simmer Down* was a success in Jamaica. Which fact proves this?

_____

4 In a shooting incident …

   a) ☐ Marley's wife was killed.

   b) ☐ Marley and his wife were hurt.

   c) ☐ Marley's manager was killed.

5 In England …

   a) ☐ Bob Marley became a songwriter.

   b) ☐ Bob Marley had to cook his own meals.

   c) ☐ Bob Marley formed a new band, 'Exodus'.

6 Why was Bob Marley a controversial figure?

a) _____

b) _____

7 After Bob Marley discovered that he had cancer ...

a) ☐ he took his doctor's advice and stopped touring.

b) ☐ he continued touring for three years.

c) ☐ he was treated in a hospital in Milan, in Italy.

8 Why was Bob Marley's death on his last journey especially tragic?

_____

Leseverstehen – *Reading*

1. Ablauf und Bewertung der Prüfung

Erster Prüfungsteil

Das **Leseverstehen** gehört – zusammen mit dem Hörverstehen – zum **ersten Prüfungsteil**, für den du insgesamt 40 Minuten (+ zehn Minuten Bonuszeit zur Orientierung oder zum Überprüfen) zur Verfügung hast. Wenn du mit diesem Pensum (Hörverstehen und Leseverstehen) früher fertig bist, hast du entsprechend mehr Zeit für den zweiten Prüfungsteil (Wortschatz und Schreiben).

Ablauf beim Leseverstehen

In diesem Teil der Prüfung liest du einen Text. Dann bearbeitest du Aufgaben zum Text.

Bewertung beim Leseverstehen

Auch beim Leseverstehen sind Wörterbücher nicht erlaubt. Bei deinen Antworten werden Rechtschreib- und Grammatikfehler nur dann bewertet, wenn man nicht mehr verstehen kann, was du geschrieben hast. Das Leseverstehen macht 15 % deiner Gesamtnote aus.

2. Typische Aufgabenformate in NRW

Im Folgenden lernst du die typischen Textsorten und Aufgabentypen kennen, die dich bei der Zentralprüfung im Bereich Leseverstehen erwarten. Die Aufgaben beziehen sich auf einen Sachtext *(Australia's Stolen Generations)*, einen fiktionalen Text *(Kasun)* und einen Comicstrip.
Die Tipp-Kästen enthalten nützliche Strategien, um mit typischen Schwierigkeiten umzugehen.

Australia's Stolen Generations

The following texts are from a museum about Aboriginal people in Australia.

Auswahlaufgaben *(Multiple choice)*

> In the mid-20th century the Australian government adopted a new policy known as the indigenous child removal policy and officials began to take Aboriginal children away from their mothers and fathers, usually by force.
> This was the fate of over 250,000 Aboriginal children, some say as many as 500,000, who had to leave their homes.

- *First read the text.*
- *Then tick the correct box.*

Tipp

Bei *Multiple choice*-Aufgaben werden einzelne Wörter aus dem Lesetext oft ersetzt durch:
- **Synonyme** (Wörter mit ähnlicher Bedeutung, wie *pretty – beautiful)*
- **Antonyme** (Wörter mit gegensätzlicher Bedeutung, wie *pretty – ugly)*

Dieses Wissen kann dir helfen, die richtige Lösung zu finden, z. B. hier:
- Zu *die* und *disease* in Lösung a) gibt es im Text keine Synonyme oder Antonyme. Lösung a) kannst du also wahrscheinlich ausschließen.
- Zu *remove* und *parents* in Lösung b) gibt es im Text Synonyme, nämlich _____ und _____. Lösung b) könnte also die richtige Lösung sein.
- Zu *stay* in Lösung c) gibt es im Text einen Gegensatz, nämlich _____. Lösung c) ist daher wahrscheinlich auch falsch.

Thousands of Aboriginal Australian children ...

a) ☐ died of disease.

b) ☐ were removed from their parents.

c) ☐ were forced to stay with their parents.

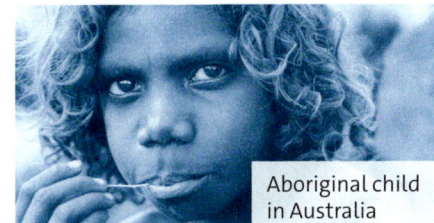

Aboriginal child in Australia

Einsetzaufgaben *(Fill in the gap)*

> The children from Aboriginal families were housed in new English-speaking homes where they were not allowed to speak their own language. And they were given the typical foods of white Australians, even though they weren't used to it.

- *First read the text.*
- *Then complete the sentences.*

Tipp

Die Struktur des Satzanfangs, den du ergänzen musst, kann dich dazu zwingen
- die **Informationen** aus dem Text **umzudrehen**:

im Text:	deine Antwort:
The children (...) were not allowed to speak their own language.	*They had to speak* _____ .

- einen **Passivsatz** in einen **Aktivsatz** umzuwandeln (oder umgekehrt):

im Text:	deine Antwort:
... they were given the typical foods of white Australians ...	*They had to* _____ *the typical foods of white Australians.*

Describe what the Aboriginal children had to do in their new homes.

a) They had to _____ .

b) And they had to _____ .

Richtig/Falsch-Aufgaben mit Begründung *(True/False – with reasons)*

> The parents were not told where their children were, and the children were not allowed to have any contact with their parents. The result was that all contact with their families, their language, their music and their way of life was broken off.

- *First read the text.*
- *Decide if the statement is true or false and tick the correct box. Then finish the sentence. You can quote from the text.*

In time, Aboriginal Australians lost touch with their culture.

This statement is ...

☐ true   ☐ false

... because the text says ...

_____

Tipp

Wichtig:
- Heißt es in der Aufgabenstellung *Quote from the text*, so <u>musst</u> du wörtlich aus dem Text zitieren.
- Steht in der Aufgabenstellung *You can quote from the text,* so kannst du wörtlich aus dem Text zitieren <u>oder</u> deine Antwort frei formulieren.

Tipp

Achte auf **Sammelbegriffe**, die stellvertretend für eine Reihe von Beispielen verwendet werden können:

im Text:	in der Aufgabe:
families, language, music, way of life	Sammelbegriff: _ _ _ _ _ _ _

Außerdem gibt es hier eine **synonyme Formulierung**:

im Text:	in der Aufgabe:
... contact with their (...) was broken off	_ _ _ _ _ _ _ _ _ _ _

Also kann das *statement* nur _____ sein.

Kasun

The following text is from a story about Kasun, a boy who lives in Sri Lanka. In this extract, Kasun writes about his first day at a new school.

Zuordnungsaufgaben (Matching)

On the first day at my new school in Colombo I was scared stiff. Not that I showed it, of course. I pretended to be relaxed while, all the time, my knees were like jelly.

My mum appeared to be calm, but I knew her better than that. Her red eyes told their own story.

5

When I got to school, all the other kids in Grade 9 seemed to know each other, maybe because they all lived in Colombo. Even the teachers had the same accent as they did. But I was from Kuruwita, a smaller town outside the capital, and I felt like

10   a fish out of water.

> **Tipp**
>
> Vorsicht! Die Sätze müssen nicht nur inhaltlich stimmen, sondern auch grammatikalisch zusammenpassen.
>
> Beispiel für eine **falsche Zuordnung**:
>
> *On his first day of school Kasun felt …*
>
> +
>
> *… was frightened.*
>
> Kasun hatte Angst – das stimmt inhaltlich. Aber die beiden Satzteile passen grammatikalisch nicht zusammen – also ist es keine richtige Zuordnung!

- First read the text.
- Then match the beginnings of sentences 1–5 with the endings A–F. You won't need one ending.

1	On his first day of school Kasun felt …	A	like most of the students.
2	Before going to school Kasun acted …	B	as though he was calm.
3	Kasun's mum had …	C	was frightened.
4	The other kids at school …	D	certainly all knew each other.
5	The teachers spoke …	E	out of place.
		F	probably cried.

- Read the text again.
- Then match the expressions from the text (1–3) with one of the feelings (A–G).

		A	cold
		B	nervous
1	"I was scared stiff."	C	tired
2	"My knees were like jelly."	D	uncomfortable
3	"I felt like a fish out of water."	E	frightened
		F	crazy
		G	bored

> **Tipp**
>
> Denke an den Sinn hinter den Wörtern, also an die Bedeutung des gesamten Ausdrucks. Beispiel:
>
> *I felt like a fish out of water.*
>
> Kasun fühlte sich nicht plötzlich wie ein Fisch!
>
> *fish out of water* ist ein Bild dafür, dass er sich
>
> _____ fühlte.

Kurzantwort-Aufgaben *(Giving short answers)*

"Hey, what's your name?"

I turned round and saw a big boy. He was smiling. But was he talking to me? Or to somebody behind me? I didn't dare answer.

⁵ "Hey, what's the problem?" said the boy, and took a step closer to me. I couldn't help but see his big hands. Was he going to hit me? "Do you think I'm going to bite you? Hi. I'm Sahan."

"I ... I'm Kasun," I stuttered. "I'm not from Colombo. I'm from Kuruwita, but I ..." ¹⁰

"Hey, calm down, you're talking too fast," laughed Sahan.

> • *Now read a second extract from* Kasun.
> • *Then answer the questions (1–3).*

1 Why doesn't Kasun answer the big boy's first question?

_____

2 What does Kasun think when the big boy comes nearer to him?

_____

3 How do we know that Kasun doesn't feel relaxed?

_____

> **Tipp**
>
> Gib bei Kurzantwort-Aufgaben deine Antwort(en) in deinen eigenen Worten – dafür bekommst du mehr Punkte! Du brauchst nicht Wort für Wort aus dem Lesetext zu zitieren. Es kann aber helfen, die relevante Stelle im Text zu markieren.

Cartoon strip

This is a cartoon strip from a youth magazine.

Sequenzierungsaufgaben *(Put in the right order)*

> **Tipp**
>
> Bei dieser Art Aufgabe ist es wichtig, zunächst den Anfang des Textes zu finden.
>
> Hier: *it* im ersten Satz von **C** *(He doesn't know about it.)* bezieht sich auf etwas, das schon gesagt wurde. Also kann **C** nicht das erste Bild sein.
>
> Achte auch auf die Bilder: Die Personen sprechen abwechselnd. Dies kann dir helfen, die Reihenfolge zu bestimmen.

> • *Look at the three pictures from a cartoon strip and read the speech bubbles.*
> • *Put the pictures A, B and C in the right order.*

Picture 1: _____   Picture 2: _____   Picture 3: _____

3. Umgang mit Verständnisproblemen

Die Lesetexte in der Zentralprüfung enthalten manchmal Wörter, die du nicht kennst, und ein Wörterbuch ist nicht erlaubt. Aber keine Angst! Mit den richtigen Strategien kannst du die Aufgaben oft trotzdem richtig lösen. Wenn du auf ein unbekanntes Wort triffst, kannst du es zunächst markieren und versuchen, es dir zu erschließen, z. B. aus dem Zusammenhang oder durch ähnliche Wörter, die du kennst. Bei einigen Aufgaben genügt es auch, wenn du die allgemeine Aussage des Textes verstehst, selbst wenn du nicht jedes Wort kennst. Dieses Kapitel präsentiert einige wichtige Strategien anhand eines Sachtextes über die Everglades.

The Everglades

The Everglades are a region of tropical wetlands in southern Florida. This text is taken from a local government brochure that gives the reasons why there will be road works on an important road in the Everglades.

- *Read the text.*
- *Then do the tasks (1–4).*

Neu – kannst du den Sinn aus bekannten Wörtern erschließen? Vielleicht ist es aber für deine Antwort auch unwichtig!

Vielleicht neu – aber du kannst es aus dem Zusammenhang erschließen: <u>Umwelt/Lebensraum</u> der Alligatoren ist in Gefahr.

Neu – aber aus dem Zusammenhang kannst du schließen: Die Haustiere sind in den Everglades, weil die Menschen sie <u>herausgelassen</u> haben.

Du kennst *wet* und *land*. Was könnten also *wetlands* sein?

1 The wetlands of the Everglades in the south of the state of Florida are famous for their alligators, snakes, turtles and other wildlife, which tourists can sometimes catch sight of from airboats or on specially-provided hiking trails. Visitor centres show alligators feeding and inform tourists about how the alligators' environment is endangered.

2 In fact, the Everglades are facing huge environmental issues. Its lakes and rivers are polluted by dirty waste water from the city of Miami. And pets released into the Everglades by inhabitants of the city have become a danger to the original wildlife.

3 But the biggest headache of all is that the wetlands are drying out. This is partly because, in the 1960s, the slow-flowing Kissimmee River was replaced by a dead straight canal that makes the water flow away too quickly. And what makes it worse is that the U.S. Highway 41, which was completed in 1928, cuts through 275 miles of the Everglades from east to west on a wall of earth. This prevents water from flowing into the southern part of the Everglades.

4 It has now been decided that parts of the canal will be filled in to allow the water to flow into the slower river. And a mile-long stretch of Highway 41 will be made into a bridge to allow water to pass under it.

Neu – aber du kennst *danger* = Gefahr.

Neues Verb – aber du kennst *dry* = trocken.

Neu – aber aus dem Zusammenhang kannst du schließen: Dieser Erdwall <u>hindert</u> das Wasser am Fließen.

1 Match the paragraphs (1–4) with the topics (A–E).
You won't need one topic.

paragraph 1	**A**	The beauty of the Everglades
paragraph 2	**B**	Pollution problems
paragraph 3	**C**	Educating the public
paragraph 4	**D**	What is being done to help
	E	Past mistakes

Tipp

Bei solchen Aufgaben geht es darum, dass du den Text im Großen und Ganzen verstehst, selbst wenn du nicht jedes Wort kennst.

Hier kannst du z. B. *topic* **B** zuordnen, selbst wenn du *pollution* nicht kennst:
1. In zwei Absätzen geht es um Probleme, nämlich __ und __. So grenzt du die Auswahl ein.
2. Zu einem dieser beiden Absätze (Absatz __) passt auch ein anderes *topic*. Es geht dabei um die Vergangenheit.

Also gehört *topic* **B** wahrscheinlich zu *paragraph* __.

2 What do visitors do in the visitor centres?
Give **two** examples.

a) They _____ .

b) They _____ .

Tipp

Hier musst du das, was im Text steht, nur leicht umformulieren, damit es zum vorgegebenen Satzanfang passt.

3 How do the people of Miami cause problems for wildlife in the Everglades?

a) They _____ .

b) They _____ .

Tipp

Im Text stehen diese Informationen im Passiv. Hier musst du Sätze im Aktiv formulieren.

4 Highway 41

a) Draw the present position of the Highway 41 on the map of the Everglades.

Now complete the following sentences:

b) The government wants to _____

_____ .

c) This will be better because _____

_____ .

Tipp

Die Regierung möchte Teile des Kanals wieder auffüllen – das stimmt, ist aber hier trotzdem nicht die richtige Antwort! Warum nicht?

Schau noch mal auf die Überschrift zu Aufgabe **4**. Worum muss es bei **b)** und **c)** also gehen?

→ Lies immer Titel und Arbeitsanweisung genau!

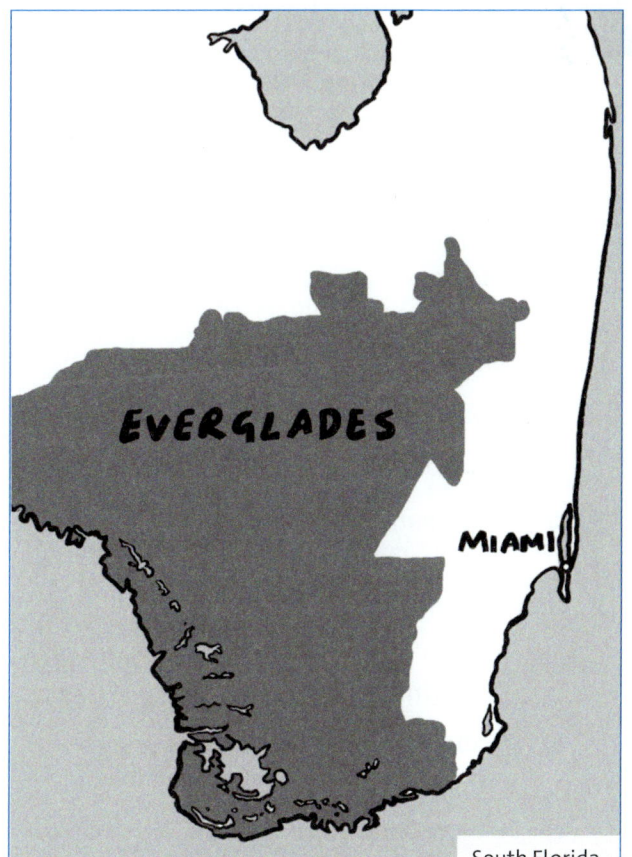

South Florida

4. Leseverstehen – *Now you*

In diesem Kapitel kannst du die Strategien, die du auf den letzten Seiten kennen gelernt hast, bei ausgewählten Aufgaben zum Leseverstehen gezielt üben. Grundlage dafür sind ein Artikel über die Filmindustrie in Neuseeland, ein Blog über ein Motorrad-Rennen auf der Isle of Man sowie ein Zeitungsartikel über indische Küche in Großbritannien.

Filming in New Zealand

This text is taken from an article in a film magazine.

Auswahlaufgaben *(Multiple choice)*

New Zealand's breathtaking landscape has long attracted the world's top film directors.

The *Lord of the Rings* trilogy, for example, was filmed in different areas of New Zealand, 5 mainly, though not exclusively, in the country's national parks. The films made use of spectacular mountains such as Mount Ngauruhoe, a treeless live volcano, and of rivers, lakes and wild canyons. But scenes were also filmed in the 10 softer and less dramatic looking green hills near Matamata. One of the advantages of filming in New Zealand is that the population density is so low, with only four and half million people in a country more or less the same size as the United 15 Kingdom (population: 64 million). So there are fewer buildings, roads and power lines to spoil the views of open countryside.

However, New Zealand's cities have also featured in films. In the film *King Kong*, for ex-20 ample, many of the scenes supposedly set in

The Lord of the Rings – The Fellowship of the Ring (USA/NZ 2001)

New York were actually filmed in Wellington, New Zealand's capital, though not its largest city. This means that the southernmost capital city in the world has a thriving film industry and professional experience of working with 25 some leading film directors.

> • *First read the text.*
> • *Then do the tasks (1–4). Tick the correct box.*

1 The *Lord of the Rings* trilogy was filmed in …

a) ☐ various regions of New Zealand.

b) ☐ national parks only.

c) ☐ one part of New Zealand.

3 New Zealand has …

a) ☐ fewer people per square kilometre than the United Kingdom.

b) ☐ about as many people per square kilometre as the United Kingdom.

c) ☐ more people per square kilometre than the United Kingdom.

2 The scenes of the film were filmed …

a) ☐ in wild hills near Matamata.

b) ☐ in spectacular and less spectacular scenery.

c) ☐ on a volcano famous for its trees.

4 Wellington …

a) ☐ is New Zealand's biggest city.

b) ☐ is further south than any other capital city in the world.

c) ☐ has good scenery but no local film industry.

The Isle of Man TT race

The Isle of Man is a small island between Britain and Ireland. It is famous for its motorcycle racing.

This text is from a blog written by a resident of the Isle of Man.

Tourist Trophy race, Isle of Man (2015)

Richtig/Falsch-Aufgaben mit Begründung *(True/False – with reasons)*

I live on one of Europe's quietest islands – the Isle of Man, set in the Irish Sea about halfway between England and Ireland. We have beautiful unspoilt countryside, narrow country roads, and every May or June we have the TT (Tourist Trophy) race. It's one of the most famous motorcycle racing events in the world, and the amazing thing is that it takes place on about 50 kilometres of our narrow public lanes.

Every year the roads are closed to the public for a week of practice runs followed by a week of racing. That means a fortnight of road chaos on the island, when it's hard for locals to get from one part of the island to another.

The only way you can bring your motorbike is by ferry, and in 2015 about 36,000 fans travelled to the Isle of Man, bringing more than 14,000 motorbikes with them – an increase of 17 % compared to the year before.

The TT has run every year since 1907, with the exception of the years during the First and Second World Wars. It has not always been popular with racers, however. Between 1907 and 2015 no less than 246 people have lost their lives during the event – 141 competitors and 105 spectators and other members of the public. As a result, the event was boycotted by a number of leading motorbike riders and sponsors in the early 1970s.

The event is a huge boost to the island's economy, but not everybody is in favour of it. I, for one, am not a motorbike fan, and I hate the crowds and the noise. But I have learned to deal with it: I just book my holidays while the racing takes place. That way, I avoid the bustle while I sunbathe on a beach in Turkey or Spain, and I pay for my holiday by letting my little house to TT visitors.

- *First read the text.*
- *Then do the tasks (1–5). Tick the correct box and quote from the text.*

1 In the TT event, the motorbikes race on a specially made track.

This statement is … ☐ true ☐ false … because the text says …

_____

2 During the TT race, roads on the Isle of Man can't be used for two weeks.

This statement is … ☐ true ☐ false … because the text says …

_____

3 The number of motorbikes brought to the Isle of Man in 2015 was higher than 2014.

This statement is … ☐ true ☐ false … because the text says …

_____

4 In the early 1970s there were no TT races.

This statement is … ☐ true ☐ false … because the text says …

5 The writer only sees disadvantages in the TT event.

This statement is … ☐ true ☐ false … because the text says …

Indian food in Britain

Gemischte Aufgabenformate *(Mixed tasks)*

Indian cooking has been popular in Britain for a long time. Britain's first Indian restaurant opened its doors in 1810, and in 1774 a British cookery book contained recipes for Indian dishes. Many British people were familiar with Indian food because Britain ruled large parts of India, and British soldiers, administrators, engineers and their families spent many years of their lives in India. They grew to like Indian food and wanted more of it when they returned to Britain.

It wasn't easy, back then, to get hold of fresh Indian spices. If they were imported from India, they could spend up to six months in transport by sea, by which time they had often lost their flavour. So people experimented with herbs and spices from the Mediterranean or from Latin America, and slowly the 'Indian' dishes in Britain began to differ from the originals in India.

What was easy to buy in Britain was a yellow powder called *curry powder*, which is a mix of dried herbs and spices. And the many individual flavourful dishes served in India came to be replaced by one standard dish called *curry*. In India, in contrast, you can't buy *curry*. It would be as absurd as asking for a soup in Europe without saying what sort of soup you want.

In the early 20th century, immigration from India increased. Many immigrants were seamen who worked on British ships and decided to stay in Britain when their ships returned to India. Some of them opened small restaurants. They were often from countries now known as Bangladesh and Pakistan, which, back then, were all part of British India, so their food was called Indian food. India became an independent country in 1948, and Pakistan and Bangladesh later split off from India to become independent countries too. Today, well over half of all Indian restaurants in Britain have Bangladeshi owners and workers – but they are usually still called Indian.

The cafe owners soon realized that nobody in Britain was selling hot food late at night. They realized that people walking home after a drink in the pub or from a late shift at work were only too happy to buy hot food. These customers did not have time to sit down and eat; they wanted their food in a form that they could carry home. This was the birth of the Indian take-away.

For years, *chicken tikka masala* was the most popular dish served in Indian take-aways. But a recent trend is that customers are becoming more adventurous and trying out a wider range of dishes. This is partly due to the influence of TV food programmes and comments on social media: customers are now more informed about the range of food available. It also reflects people's concerns about their own health, with many customers looking for lower-calory dishes.

- *First read the text.*
- *Then do the tasks (1–6).*
- *For tasks 1 and 3 tick the correct box.*
- *For tasks 2 and 4 complete the sentences.*
- *For tasks 5 and 6 decide if the statements are true or false and tick the correct box.*
  Then finish the sentences. You can quote from the text.

1 A British book from 1774 …

   a) ☐ warned its readers against eating Indian food.

   b) ☐ told its readers how to prepare Indian food.

   c) ☐ explained how to open an Indian restaurant.

2 Many British people liked Indian food in Britain 200 years ago because …

_____

3 Herbs and spices that were imported from India …

   a) ☐ were often too expensive.

   b) ☐ often did not have much taste.

   c) ☐ were too spicy for people in Britain.

4 You can't buy *curry* in India because …

_____

5 Indian restaurants are often not really Indian.

   This statement is … ☐ true ☐ false … because the text says …

_____

6 People are now increasingly buying the same food in Indian take-aways.

   This statement is … ☐ true ☐ false … because the text says …

_____

Wortschatz – *Vocabulary*

1. Ablauf und Bewertung der Prüfung

Zweiter Prüfungsteil

Im **zweiten Prüfungsteil** geht es um **Wortschatz und Schreiben**. Für diese beiden Fertigkeiten hast du 80 Minuten Zeit und ggf. noch zehn Minuten Bonuszeit, sofern du sie nicht schon im ersten Prüfungsteil eingesetzt hast.

Ablauf beim Wortschatz

Im Abschnitt **Wortschatz** liest du zunächst Sätze, die inhaltlich miteinander verbunden sind. In jedem Satz zeigt eine Lücke, wo ein Wort fehlt. Deine Aufgabe besteht darin, ein passendes Wort für jede Lücke zu finden – mal mit *Multiple choice*-Auswahl, mal ohne. Außerdem können dir im Abschnitt Wortschatz auch *Matching*-Aufgaben begegnen, bei denen du z. B. Synonyme, Gegensätze oder Umschreibungen zuordnen musst, oder Aufgaben, bei denen du Wörter zu einem vorgegebenen Thema ergänzt, z. B. in Form eines Wörternetzes.

Bewertung beim Wortschatz

Der Bereich Wortschatz macht 10 % deiner Gesamtnote aus.

2. Typische Aufgabenformate in NRW

Im Folgenden lernst du die typischen Aufgabentypen kennen, die dich bei der Zentralprüfung im Bereich Wortschatz erwarten. Die Aufgaben beziehen sich auf die Themen Ernährung und Gesundheit.
Die Tipp-Kästen enthalten nützliche Hinweise und Hilfen.

Healthy eating

The following text is from a brochure about healthy eating.

Auswahlaufgaben *(Multiple choice)*

> • *Tick the correct box. There is only one correct answer.*

In terms of health, we all know the ...

    a) ☐ enthusiasm **b)** ☐ importance

    c) ☐ influence   **d)** ☐ connections

of eating the right kinds of food.

Tipp

Lies die Sätze gut durch. Sie geben dir einen Zusammenhang, der dir hilft, das richtige Wort zu wählen.
Bei manchen Aufgaben hilft dir – neben dem Textverständnis – auch dein Weltwissen. Hier:

- Du weißt, dass es hier um *health* (Gesundheit) und *food* (Essen) geht.
- Was weißt du über den Zusammenhang zwischen Gesundheit und Essen? Dass es wichtig ist!
- Du kennst *important* = wichtig.

Die richtige Lösung ist also

_____.

Your body …

a) ☐ benefits   **b)** ☐ demands   **c)** ☐ prevents   **d)** ☐ accepts

from eating at least five portions of fruit and vegetables every day.

> **Tipp**
>
> Nur eins dieser vier Verben kann hier die Präposition *from* nach sich ziehen. Weißt du, welches?

Einsetzaufgaben *(Fill in the gap)*

> • *Fill in suitable words.*

Healthy eating doesn't mean you have to _____ sugary foods completely, but it means that you should eat less of them.

> **Tipp**
>
> • Bei Einsetzaufgaben sind oft mehrere Lösungen möglich. Du musst dich aber für **eine** entscheiden, denn du bekommst **keinen** Punkt, wenn du mehr als eine Antwort in die Lücke schreibst.
>
> • Achte auf die Satzstruktur – sie kann deine Gedanken in die richtige Richtung lenken. Hier:
>
> *It doesn't mean …, but it means …* = **ein Gegensatz.**
>
> Du brauchst süßes Essen nicht komplett _____ , aber du solltest weniger davon essen.
>
> Welche englischen Wörter kennst du für aufgeben/vermeiden/verweigern/…?

Zuordnungsaufgaben *(Matching)*

> • *Match the health words (1–10) with the definitions (A–J).*

1	sick	**A**	a person who works at a hospital
2	first aid	**B**	an unusual reaction to certain foods, plants or animals
3	flu	**C**	an object that is used to measure body temperature
4	nurse	**D**	another word for sickness
5	paramedic	**E**	not in good health, suffering from an illness
6	fever	**F**	a disease that causes fever, pain and weakness
7	allergy	**G**	to have air come suddenly and noisily through your nose
8	thermometer	**H**	a person who is trained to give emergency medical treatment
9	to sneeze	**I**	body temperature above the normal temperature
10	disease	**J**	simple medical treatment in an emergency

> **Tipp**
>
> • Keine Panik, wenn du ein Wort nicht kennst! Manchmal hilft dir schon die Wortart weiter. Hier gibt es z. B. nur ein Verb, nämlich _____ . Also kann die passende Definition dafür nur _____ sein.
>
> • Manche englischen Wörter sind ähnlich wie deutsche Wörter, z. B. *thermometer* und *temperature*. Das hilft dir, den Begriff **8** mit Definition _____ zu verbinden.

Ergänzungsaufgaben

- *Fill the network with ten health words.*
- *Write at least one word for each box.*
- *Don't write more than four words for any box.*

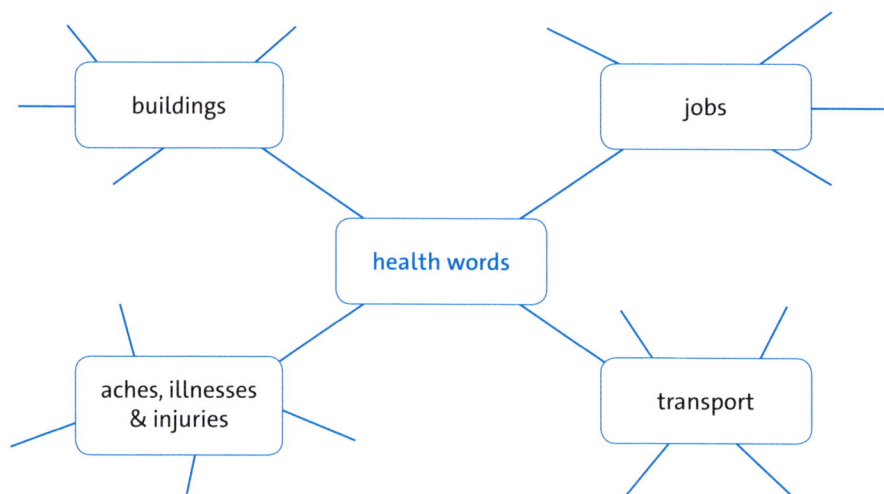

3. Wortschatz – *Now you*

Nun kannst du die Aufgabentypen und Strategien, die du auf den letzten Seiten kennen gelernt hast, bei ausgewählten Wortschatz-Aufgaben gezielt üben. Grundlage dafür sind eine Broschüre über gesunde Ernährung sowie ein Zeitungsartikel über Teenager als Konsumenten.

Healthy eating

Auswahlaufgaben *(Multiple choice)*

- *Tick the correct box. There is only one correct answer.*

1   Eat the right kind of food and be more active if you want to …

   a) ☐ lose   **b)** ☐ leave   **c)** ☐ receive   **d)** ☐ miss

   weight.

2   Breakfast is an important meal, so you shouldn't miss it even if you're …

   a) ☐ thirsty.   **b)** ☐ hungry.   **c)** ☐ relaxed.   **d)** ☐ in a hurry.

3 Try to eat a range of foods because your body ...

a) ☐ consumes **b)** ☐ needs **c)** ☐ refuses **d)** ☐ consists of

different minerals and vitamins.

4 Fruit and vegetables are usually ...

a) ☐ more frozen **b)** ☐ more comfortable **c)** ☐ cheaper **d)** ☐ weaker

when they're in season.

5 And don't forget to drink. The government ...

a) ☐ offers **b)** ☐ recommends **c)** ☐ receives **d)** ☐ reports

six to eight glasses a day of water, milk or other drinks.

Teenagers as customers

Einsetzaufgaben *(Fill in the gap)*

> • *Fill in suitable words.*

1 A majority of teenagers have money and most

of them are prepared to make their own _____ when they buy things.

2 And while their parents tend to stay with the brands that they have used for years, teenagers are

willing to _____.

3 What's more, a growing _____ of teenagers are passing their

old phones and tablets on to their parents, bringing the older generation into the market.

4 These two facts make teenagers very _____ to the companies

that bring new technological products to the market.

5 But companies that wish to _____ their products to teenagers

have to know this market really well.

6 For the fact is that teenagers are not lazy customers. On the contrary, they will do research and read

reviews to get the best deal and make _____ that they get

value for money.

Schreiben – *Writing*

1. Ablauf und Bewertung der Prüfung

Zweiter Prüfungsteil

Das **Schreiben** gehört – zusammen mit dem Wortschatz – zum **zweiten Prüfungsteil**, für den du insgesamt 80 Minuten (+ eventuell noch nicht genutzte Bonuszeit von bis zu zehn Minuten) zur Verfügung hast.

Ablauf beim Schreiben

Dieser Teil der Prüfung besteht aus drei Teilaufgaben:

1. Du liest einen Text. Dann beschreibst du den Inhalt des Textes oder eines Textteils gemäß Aufgabenstellung in deinen eigenen Worten.

2. Du erläuterst die Meinungen, Gefühle, Entwicklung oder Veränderung einer oder mehrerer Hauptpersonen des Lesetextes.

3. Du schreibst einen eigenen längeren Text. Hier hast du die Wahl zwischen zwei Alternativen:

    a: Du schreibst einen argumentativen Text (z. B. *comment*, *discussion*) zum Thema des Lesetextes.

    b: Du schreibst einen kreativen Text (z. B. Perspektivwechsel, Fortsetzung, alternatives Ende, Umschreiben in ein anderes Textformat) oder einen beschreibenden, berichtenden oder erzählenden Text (z. B. Erfahrungsbericht, Erlebnisbericht, Tagebucheintrag, E-Mail), der mit der Thematik des Lesetextes zu tun hat.

Bewertung beim Schreiben

Das Schreiben macht 60 % deiner Gesamtnote aus und ist somit der wichtigste Bestandteil der Prüfung. Die insgesamt 72 Punkte beim Schreiben werden für **Inhalt** und **Sprache** vergeben.

Der **Inhalt** im Prüfungsteil Schreiben zählt 25 % deiner Gesamtnote. So werden die Punkte verteilt:
*   Teilaufgabe 1: 8 Punkte
*   Teilaufgabe 2: 10 Punkte
*   Teilaufgabe 3a oder 3b: 12 Punkte

Diese Punktzahlen siehst du auf deinem Prüfungsbogen.

Die **Sprache** im Prüfungsteil Schreiben zählt 35 % deiner Gesamtnote. Diese Punkte werden nicht pro Teilaufgabe vergeben, sondern für deine Schreibleistung als Ganzes. Folgende Kriterien tragen zu dieser Note bei:

*   **Kommunikation:** Punkte dafür, dass du ...
    *   verständlich und lesbar schreibst,
    *   deine Gedanken sinnvoll ordnest und dich nicht wiederholst,
    *   die üblichen Regeln für die Textsorte (Brief, Geschichte, Kommentar etc.) beachtest.

*   **Ausdrucksvermögen:** Punkte dafür, dass du ...
    *   in deinen eigenen Worten schreibst und eine Vielfalt an Worten gebrauchst,
    *   nicht ganze Sätze aus dem Text abschreibst, sondern die Wörter des Texts in deine Formulierungen einbindest,
    *   komplexe Sätze bildest (mit Haupt- und Nebensätzen, *linking words*, *time phrases* etc.)

*   **Sprachliche Korrektheit:** Punkte dafür, dass du ...
    *   die Wörter richtig schreibst,
    *   die Grammatik beherrschst.

Diese Punktzahlen siehst du <u>nicht</u> auf deinem Prüfungsbogen.

2. Typische Aufgabenformate in NRW

Im Folgenden lernst du die typischen Aufgabenformate kennen, die dich bei der Zentralprüfung im Bereich Schreiben erwarten. Die Aufgaben beziehen sich auf einen Blog-Text zum Thema Wochenendjobs für Jugendliche. Die Tipp-Kästen enthalten nützliche Hinweise und Hilfen.

My weekend job

Sarah (16) is in trouble with her parents because of her weekend job. She writes about this in her blog.

- *Read the tasks carefully.*
- *Write complete sentences.*
- *Make sure to write about all the aspects presented in each task.*

I hate asking my parents for money. OK, they give me pocket money, but it's never enough for what I need. I pay for my clothes, the contract for my mobile phone, and for a pizza and a drink when I go out with my friends – but that all costs more than what my parents give me every week. That's why I got a job.

It's only a weekend job – and usually I work on Saturday or Sunday, but not both – so I still have time to do homework. I work in a clothes shop in town and I really enjoy it. I have to be there early because I help to clean and organize the shop before the customers arrive. Then I help customers to find what they want and sometimes I even take payment at the till. I'm taking on more responsibility than I have ever had before, and my boss has praised me for being a reliable worker: she knows that I have never arrived late for work.

So you would have thought that my parents would be happy. I'm going out into the adult world, I'm showing that I'm responsible and well-organized, and of course I don't have to ask them for money so often.

I'm really happy about all that. But my parents aren't. They constantly complain about my job.

First they say that I won't do my homework, or that I'll be too tired for school on Monday mornings – even though no teacher has complained about my work. Then they say that the music in the shop is too loud and that working there will destroy my hearing. They have also pointed out that we sell cheap clothes that have been made in Bangladesh, where men, women and children often work in terrible conditions for very little pay. They would prefer it, they say, if I worked in a fair-trade shop that sends more money back to the workers who make the products.

But I have to work where people give me a job, don't I? They forget that I applied for loads of different jobs for about three months without any success. I didn't *choose* to work in this shop – it was the only job offer I got. And anyway, if I worked in a fair-trade shop, I'd be just as tired on a Monday morning, wouldn't I?

I think the real problem is that my parents just can't accept that I'm not a little child any more. They want to control everything I do, and they're afraid that I'll be too independent if I earn my own money. This is the first time we have argued like this – we usually have a good relationship! But I'm determined to keep my job.

Aufgabe zur Sicherung des Textverständnisses

 Describe what you get to know about Sarah and the problem that she has with her parents.

Wie könnte deine Lösung aussehen?
Hier ist ein Beispiel. Lies den Text und die Tipps dazu.
Dann streiche die falschen Alternativen durch.

Tipp

Mache kurze Notizen oder markiere die Stellen im Text, z. B.

- *what I know about Sarah:*
  - *at school*
  - *needs money: phone, clothes …*
  - *…*

- *what I know about the problem: parents against her job:*
  - *less time for homework*
  - *loud music*
  - *…*

Wichtige Information – aus dem Text zu schließen

Bilde komplexe Sätze:
… *because* …
… *although* …
… *as* …
… *but* …
… *so* …
… *On the one hand* …
…

Fasse das Problem in deinen eigenen Worten zusammen.

Sarah has left school / is a student at school and she usually gets on well with / quarrels with her parents. But now she has a weekend job because/so she needs money for her clothes, her phone and for going out with her friends. She works in a clothes shop on a Saturday or Sunday, and she works hard because/ although it means she has to get up early. She arrives on time / is often late, she helps to prepare the shop and she helps the customers. Sometimes she works at the till.

Her boss has said that she is a good worker / is a bit unreliable. But Sarah's parents are unhappy with her job and want her to give it up / don't think that Sarah is a very good worker. They

But Sarah thinks that …

Diese Information kommt am Ende des Texts vor – ändere die Reihenfolge.

Formuliere eigenständig, z. B. andersherum als im Text: *never late → ?*

Schreibe noch nichts über Sarahs Meinungen oder Gefühle.

Aufgabe zur grundlegenden Interpretation

 Explain Sarah's and her parents' feelings about her job and Sarah's opinion about her parents' reaction.

Tipp

Lies die Arbeitsanweisungen immer <u>genau</u> durch, damit du <u>genau</u> weißt, worüber du schreiben sollst.

a) Zu welchen drei Themen solltest du dich in deiner Antwort äußern?

1 ☐ what Sarah feels about her job

2 ☐ what Sarah feels about her parents

3 ☐ what Sarah's parents feel about her job

4 ☐ what Sarah's boss thinks about Sarah

5 ☐ what Sarah thinks about her parents' reaction

b) Mache kurze Notizen zu jedem der drei Themen, die du in **a)** angekreuzt hast.

Thema __ : *enjoys job,*

Thema __ : *worried about homework,*

Thema __ : _____

c) Wie könnte deine Lösung nun aussehen? Schreibe zu jedem Thema aus **a)** einen Absatz.

Hier ist ein Beispiel. Lies den Text und die Tipps dazu und bearbeite die Aufgaben in den Kästen.

> Sarah schreibt *enjoy*. Wie kann man das anders ausdrücken?

> In diesem Absatz werden drei Gedanken ausgeführt. Sarahs erster Gedanke ist unterstrichen. Unterstreiche die beiden anderen Gedanken.

> Zu jedem Gedanken wird ein Beispiel genannt, das den Gedanken unterstützt. Unterkringele die Beispiele zu Sarahs ersten beiden Gedanken.
> Kannst du beim dritten Gedanken das Beispiel in deinen eigenen Worten ergänzen?

Sarah really ▯▯▯▯ her job. She's grateful for the opportunity to prove that she can work well in the adult world. And of course she's happy to earn some money because she ▯▯▯▯ ▯▯▯▯ her parents for money.

But Sarah's parents ▯▯▯▯ ▯▯▯▯ that she has taken a job. They don't like the sort of clothes that she sells and say that she should work in a different kind of shop. And they're worried about her health and fear that she'll get behind with her school work and homework.

Sarah thinks that her parents' reaction is unfair: she didn't choose to work in this shop – it was the only job she could get. She also thinks they're illogical: after all, the effect on her school work would be the same if she worked in a fair-trade shop. And finally, Sarah thinks that her parents' reaction doesn't really have anything to do with her job: they're unhappy, she says, because ▯▯▯▯ ▯▯▯▯ ▯▯▯▯ .

> Wie hat Sarah das ausgedrückt?

> Sarah schreibt *hate asking*. Wie kann man das anders ausdrücken?

> Sarah schreibt *complain about my job*. Wie kann man das anders ausdrücken?

Argumentatives Schreiben

> *"Getting a weekend job while you are still at school is a stupid idea."*
>
> **3** **a)** *Comment on the statement from your point of view.*
>
> *Include the following aspects:*
> * *Give reasons in favour of and against this statement.*
> * *Give examples of situations that support your arguments.*
> * *Write a conclusion and state what you think about having a weekend job.*

Tipp

Inhalt und **Struktur** deines Kommentars sind wichtig. Vergiss aber nicht, auch auf deine **Sprache** zu achten – sie fließt sogar noch stärker in deine Note ein.

1   Mache dir Notizen zu Einleitung, Mittelteil und Schluss. Überlege dir zwei bis drei Argumente für jede Seite *(pro* und *con)* und finde Beispiele aus deinen eigenen Erfahrungen oder den Erfahrungen von Freunden. Du kannst dafür diese Tabelle benutzen.

Getting a weekend job while you are still at school is a stupid idea.		
Introduction		
	pro: job is a stupid idea	**con**: job is a good idea
Argument 1	*less time for homework*	*become independent*
Example		
Argument 2		
Example		
Argument 3		
Example		
Conclusion		

2   Nun schreibe deinen Text:
   • Beginne mit einer kurzen Einleitung, in der du darlegst, um welche Frage es geht.
   • Führe Argumente für und gegen das Statement auf und belege sie mit Beispielen:
     − Bist du **für** das Statement, beginne mit den Gründen dagegen.
     − Bist du **gegen** das Statement, beginne mit den Gründen dafür.
   • Komme zu einem zusammenfassenden Ergebnis.
   • Achte auf deine Sprache! Lies dazu noch einmal die Hinweise zur Bewertung der Sprache bei Schreibaufgaben auf S. 30.

3   Überprüfe deinen Text. Dafür kannst du diese Checkliste verwenden.

Prüfe, ob du die Aufgabenstellung erfüllt hast:	
Ich habe eine Einleitung geschrieben.	☐
Ich habe Argumente für und gegen die Aussage aufgeführt.	☐
Ich habe Beispiele für die Argumente gegeben.	☐
Ich habe eine Schlussfolgerung geschrieben.	☐

Prüfe auch die Sprache deines Textes:	
Ich habe komplexe Sätze mit Haupt- und Nebensatz gebildet.	☐
Ich habe einen breiten Wortschatz verwendet.	☐
Ich habe verschiedene grammatische Strukturen verwendet.	☐
Ich habe abwechslungsreiche Satzanfänge geschrieben.	☐
Ich habe *linking words (and, but, so, because, on the one hand, first/second/...)* verwendet.	☐
Ich habe *time words (at first, next, two hours later, during the summer ...)* verwendet.	☐
Ich habe meine Rechtschreibung überprüft.	☐
Ich habe die Grammatik überprüft.	☐

Kreatives Schreiben

"It was Sarah's first day at work and she was nervous. But then somebody really famous came in – and spoke with her. It was amazing! ..."

3 **b)** *Tell the rest of the story.*

Include the following aspects:

- *Say where Sarah worked and describe her work.*
- *Say who the famous person was and describe him/her.*
- *Write the dialogue between the famous person and Sarah.*
- *Describe why the meeting was important for Sarah.*

1 Mache zunächst Notizen.

2 Lies dieses Beispiel für einen gelungenen Textanfang. Warum werden die markierten Stellen bei der Bewertung besonders viele Punkte bringen? Ordne die Kriterien A–F den Textstellen zu.

Tipp

Notiere Ideen zu allen Punkten, die oben in der Arbeitsanweisung erwähnt sind.

Wortschatz	Grammatik	Satzstruktur
A breiter Wortschatz, bildliche Sprache	**B** Vielfalt an grammatischen Strukturen	**C** unterschiedliche Satz-anfänge **D** in den Text integrierter Dialog **E** Fragesätze **F** Nebensätze

B: Vielfalt an grammatischen Strukturen

Sarah had never wanted to work in a clothes shop, but she was really happy when she got a job in the clothes shop next to her school. Still, on her first day at work she was very nervous. Would she make some stupid mistakes? Would the other workers be nice to her?

Everything started well, but then suddenly Sarah dropped a box full of new shirts onto the floor. She went on her hands and knees to pick them up – and this was her position when the door opened and a customer came in. And to her big surprise, it was ...

... looked at Sarah and said, "Well, good morning. Have you lost something?"

3 Nun schreibe deinen Text:
- Du kannst den Textanfang aus **2** benutzen oder deinen eigenen Anfang schreiben.
- Nutze deine Notizen aus **1**.
- Achte auf deine Sprache! Lies dazu noch einmal die Hinweise zur Bewertung der Sprache bei Schreibaufgaben auf S. 30.

4 Überprüfe deinen Text. Dafür kannst du diese Checkliste verwenden.

Prüfe, ob du die Aufgabenstellung erfüllt hast:	
Ich habe Hintergrundinformationen über Sarahs Job gegeben.	☐
Ich habe die berühmte Person genannt und beschrieben.	☐
Ich habe einen kurzen Dialog in den Text integriert.	☐
Ich habe geschrieben, welche Bedeutung die Begegnung für Sarah hatte.	☐

Prüfe auch die Sprache deines Textes:	
Ich habe komplexe Sätze mit Haupt- und Nebensatz gebildet.	☐
Ich habe einen breiten Wortschatz oder bildliche Sprache verwendet.	☐
Ich habe verschiedene grammatische Strukturen verwendet.	☐
Ich habe abwechslungsreiche Satzanfänge geschrieben.	☐
Ich habe *linking words (and, but, so, because, on the one hand...)* verwendet.	☐
Ich habe *time words (at first, next, two hours later, during the summer...)* verwendet.	☐
Ich habe meine Rechtschreibung überprüft.	☐
Ich habe die Grammatik überprüft.	☐

Englisch

ABSCHLUSS-PRÜFUNGS-TRAINER

Nordrhein-Westfalen

Lösungen

Cornelsen

Hinweis zu den Lösungen:
Dieses Lösungsheft bietet Lösungen zu allen Aufgaben, verzichtet jedoch auf Lösungen zu den strategischen und oft individuellen Zwischenschritten in den Tipp-Kästen.

Calgary's skyways

Auswahlaufgaben (Multiple choice)
An underground city … **c)** *allows people to avoid the cold weather.*

Zuordnungsaufgaben (Matching)
1 Burlington: **D** · *2 Stoney Creek:* **B** · *3 Kissimmee:* **A** ·
4 Jacksonville: **F** · *5 Jasper National Park:* **E**

Einsetzaufgaben (Fill in the gap)
1 overhead · *2 downtown/central*

Kurzantwort-Aufgaben (Giving short answers)
1a) *They don't have to walk in the rain and cold. / are protected from the rain and cold. / are protected from the weather. / …*
b) *They don't have to cross the roads. / are safe from the traffic. / are safer because they never have to cross a road. / …*
2 Because there is less life in the streets. / less life at street level. / Because the streets feel deserted. / are empty. / …

Richtig/Falsch-Aufgaben (True/False)
1 false · *2 true* · *3 true*

The Niagara Falls

1c) *are for the most part in Canada.*
2 They wear clothes/coats/ponchos against the rain. / They wear waterproof ponchos/raincoats/…
3b) *was the first state park in the USA.*
4 raise money
5b) *injured.*
6a) *mainly* · *b)* *waterproof ponchos* · *c)* *the country's oldest* · *d)* *raise money* · *e)* *did hurt her head*

The Tour de Yorkshire

1c) *began in Yorkshire.*
2c) *there were old yellow bicycles on the sides of the roads used by the race.*
3b) *didn't expect the enthusiastic reaction from people in Yorkshire.*
4b) *left people in Yorkshire wanting to see more cycling races.*
5a) *includes hills that are difficult even for experienced cyclists.*

Bob Marley

1 1: B, C · *2: A, E* · *3: B, D*
2 true … because Gwen says … that this is where he became interested in music. / that this is where he formed his first band. / that Bob became interested in music there. / that Bob formed his first band there. / …
3 It was Number One in the Jamaican charts. / It was No. 1 in Jamaica. / …
4b) *Marley and his wife were hurt.*
5a) *Bob Marley became a songwriter.*
6a) *He took drugs/cannabis.*
b) *Because he got involved in politics. / fought for the independence of African countries. / Because of his role in politics. / …*
7b) *he continued touring for three years.*
8 Because he never reached Jamaica. / never saw his home country again. / died in the USA. / was so young (36 years old) when he died. / …

Australia's Stolen Generations

Auswahlaufgaben (Multiple choice)
Thousands of Aboriginal Australian children … **b)** *were removed from their parents.*

Einsetzaufgaben (Fill in the gap)
a) *speak English* · *b)* *eat the typical foods of white Australians / eat foods that they weren't used to*

Richtig-/Falsch-Aufgaben mit Begründung (True/False – with reasons)
true … because the text says … that all contact with their families, their language, their music and their way of life was broken off. / that the children weren't allowed to have any contact with their families. / …

Kasun

Zuordnungsaufgaben (Matching)
1 E · *2 B* · *3 F* · *4 D* · *5 A*

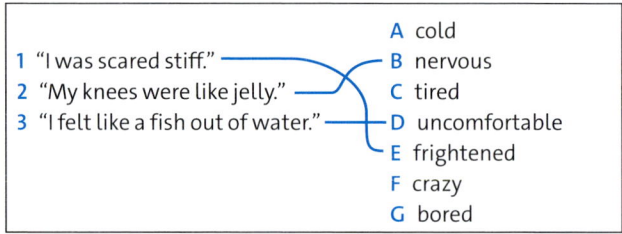

1 "I was scared stiff."	A cold
2 "My knees were like jelly."	B nervous
3 "I felt like a fish out of water."	C tired
	D uncomfortable
	E frightened
	F crazy
	G bored

Kurzantwort-Aufgaben (Giving short answers)
1 (Because) he doesn't know if the big boy is talking/speaking to him.
2 He thinks that the big boy is going to / wants to / might hit him.
3 He stutters. / He talks too fast. / Sahan tells Kasun to calm down. / …

Cartoon strip

Sequenzierungsaufgaben (Put in the right order)
Picture 1: **B** · *Picture 2:* **A** · *Picture 3:* **C**

The Everglades

1 paragraph 1: **C** · *paragraph 2:* **B** · *paragraph 3:* **E** · *paragraph 4:* **D**
2a) *watch alligator feedings / watch alligators feeding / see what alligators eat / …*
b) *learn about how the alligators' environment is endangered / find out about the dangers that exist for the alligators' environment / …*
3a) *pollute the rivers and lakes with their dirty waste water / let dirty water flow into the rivers and lakes / …*
b) *release their pets into the Everglades / let their pets run into the Everglades / allow their pets to go into the Everglades / …*
4a)

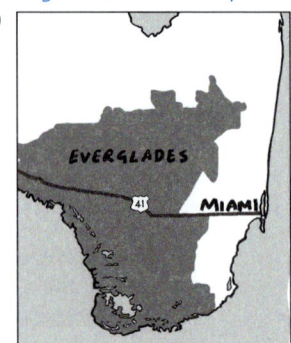

b) make a mile-long stretch of Highway 41 into a bridge / turn a part of the highway into a bridge / …
c) it allows water to pass under the bridge / water can pass underneath the bridge / water will be able to flow into the southern part of the Everglades / …

Filming in New Zealand

Auswahlaufgaben (Multiple choice)
1a) various regions of New Zealand.
2b) in spectacular and less spectacular scenery.
3a) fewer people per square kilometre than the United Kingdom.
4b) is further south than any other capital city in the world.

The Isle of Man TT race

Richtig-/Falsch-Aufgaben mit Begründung (True/False – with reasons)
1 false … because the text says … that the race "takes place on about 50 kilometres of our narrow public lanes".
2 true … because the text says … that "the roads are closed to the public for a week of practice runs followed by a week of racing".
3 true … because the text says … that there was "an increase of 17 % compared to the year before".
4 false … because the text says … that the race "was boycotted by a number of leading motorbike riders and sponsors in the early 1970s". / that "the TT has run every year since 1907, with the exception of the years during the First and Second World Wars".
5 false … because the text says … that "the event is a huge boost to the island's economy". / "I pay for my holiday by letting my little house to TT visitors".

Indian food in Britain

Gemischte Aufgabenformate (Mixed tasks)
1b) told its readers how to prepare Indian food.
2 they had lived in India for a long time. / had spent many years of their lives in India. / …
3b) often did not have much taste.
4 there are many different types of curry. / the word "curry" is too general. / not specific enough. / …
5 true … because the text says … that their owners came from countries now known as Bangladesh and Pakistan. / that the people who own the restaurants came from countries like Bangladesh and Pakistan. / …
6 false … because the text says … that customers are becoming more adventurous. / are trying out a wider range of dishes. / are more informed about the range of food available. / …

TRAINING SECTION: Wortschatz ▶ S. 26–29

Healthy eating

Auswahlaufgaben (Multiple choice)
In terms of health, we all know the … *b)* importance of eating the right kinds of food.

Your body … *a)* benefits from eating at least five portions …

Einsetzaufgaben (Fill in the gap)
Healthy eating doesn't mean you have to avoid / give up / refuse / reject sugary foods completely …

Zuordnungsaufgaben (Matching)
1 E · 2 J · 3 F · 4 A · 5 H · 6 I · 7 B · 8 C · 9 G · 10 D

Ergänzungsaufgaben
buildings: hospital, clinic, emergency room, doctor's office, gym, …
jobs: doctor, nurse, dentist, paramedic, ambulance driver, surgeon, receptionist, chemist, pharmacist, fitness trainer, …
aches, illnesses & injuries: back ache, ear ache, tooth ache, headache, stomach ache, sore throat, broken leg/arm/finger/nose, cold, flu, allergy, …
transport: ambulance, helicopter, life boat, stretcher, …

Healthy eating

Auswahlaufgaben (Multiple choice)
1a) lose · *2d)* in a hurry. · *3b)* needs · *4c)* cheaper · *5b)* recommends

Teenagers as customers

Einsetzaufgaben (Fill in the gap)
1 decisions/choices · *2* experiment/change/switch · *3* number · *4* attractive/useful/valuable · *5* sell/market · *6* sure

---

TRAINING SECTION: Schreiben ▶ S. 30–36

Hinweis zu den Lösungsvorschlägen beim Schreiben:
- Teilaufgaben 1 (Textverständnis) und 2 (Textinterpretation) stützen sich stark auf den zugrunde liegenden Lesetext. Für diese Teilaufgaben werden daher englischsprachige Lösungsbeispiele angeboten. Sie sind als Orientierungshilfe gedacht. Es sind aber auch andere (inhaltlich ähnliche) Lösungen denkbar.
- Teilaufgaben 3a (argumentatives Schreiben) und 3b (kreatives Schreiben) sind freier angelegt. Dadurch gibt es eine noch größere Bandbreite an möglichen (auch inhaltlich sehr unterschiedlichen) Lösungen. Für diese Teilaufgaben wird daher auf Deutsch skizziert, welche Aspekte dein Text beinhalten sollte.
- Inhalt und Struktur deines Textes sind wichtig, aber Sprache und Ausdruck fließen noch stärker in die Benotung ein. Achte daher auf die Hinweise zur Bewertung von Ausdruck und Sprache auf S. 30.

My weekend job

1. Aufgabe zur Sicherung des Textverständnisses
Sarah is a student at school and she usually gets on well with her parents. But now she has a weekend job because she needs money for her clothes, her phone and for going out with her friends. She works in a clothes shop on a Saturday or Sunday, and she works hard although it means she has to get up early. She arrives on time, she helps to prepare the shop and she helps the customers. Sometimes she works at the till.
Her boss has said that she is a good worker. But Sarah's parents are unhappy with her job and want her to give it up. They say that the job is bad for Sarah's health and for her progress at school. So now Sarah is in trouble with her parents.

2. Aufgabe zur grundlegenden Interpretation
a) Themen 1, 3, 5
b) Thema 1: enjoys job, likes having responsibility, takes job seriously, proud of her boss's praise, …
Thema 3: worried about homework, worried about Sarah's hearing/health, complain that the shop isn't fair-trade, …
Thema 5: thinks her parents are unfair, thinks they can't accept that she's growing up, thinks her parents are too controlling, doesn't want to give up her job for her parents, …

c) *Sarah really* likes/loves/appreciates/... *her job. She's grateful for the opportunity to prove that she can work well in the adult world. And of course she's happy to earn some money because she* doesn't like asking *her parents for money.*
But Sarah's parents aren't happy / don't think it's good / are disappointed *that she has taken a job. They don't like the sort of clothes that she sells and say that she should work in a different kind of shop. And they're worried about her health and fear that she'll get behind with her school work and homework.*
Sarah thinks that her parents' reaction is unfair: she didn't choose to work in this shop – it was the only job she could get. She also thinks they're illogical: after all, the effect on her school work would be the same if she worked in a fair-trade shop. And finally, Sarah thinks that her parents' reaction doesn't really have anything to do with her job: they're unhappy, she says, because they worry that she will become too independent if she earns her own money.

3a) Argumentatives Schreiben
Du beginnst deinen **Kommentar** mit einer kurzen, zum Thema **hinführenden Einleitung**.
Du führst zwei bis drei **Argumente für** (z. B. weniger Zeit für Hausaufgaben, Sport, Musik und Freunde, geringer Verdienst bei Schülerjobs) und **gegen** (z. B. Unabhängigkeit von den Eltern, mehr Geld, Berufserfahrung) das Statement auf und belegst sie jeweils mit **Beispielen** aus deinen eigenen Erfahrungen. Das aus deiner Sicht wichtigste Argument für deine Position kommt als letztes.
Du kommst zu einem abgewogenen, zusammenfassenden **Ergebnis**.

3b) Kreatives Schreiben
Du beschreibst, dass Sarah in einem Modeladen arbeitet, dass es ihr erster Tag ist und wie es ihr geht.
Du schilderst, was Sarah gerade tut, als die berühmte Person hereinkommt, und nennst und beschreibst diese Person.
Du gibst (eingebettet in den Text) wieder, was Sarah und die berühmte Person sagen.
Du schilderst kurz die Folgen der Begegnung und warum sie für Sarah wichtig ist. Hier kannst du z. B. Sarahs Konflikt mit ihren Eltern aufgreifen.
2
had never wanted: **B** (Vielfalt an grammatischen Strukturen) · *when she got:* **F** (Nebensätze) · *Still:* **C** (unterschiedliche Satzanfänge) · *Would she make some stupid mistakes? Would the other workers be nice to her?:* **E** (Fragesätze) · *hands and knees:* **A** (breiter Wortschatz, bildliche Sprache) · *"Well, good morning. Have you lost something?":* **D** (in den Text integrierter Dialog)

MUSTERPRÜFUNG 1: Hörverstehen ▶ S. 38–40

Bo-Kaap – a special district in Cape Town

1a) at the end of the 18th century.
2 true
3 They were forced to come and work in Cape Town. / were treated very badly / like slaves. / hardly earned anything. / ...
4b) are Asian.
5a) They worked in sugar fields. · *b)* They worked in coal mines.
6c) gives information about the Asian population of Cape Town.
7b) that the houses are brightly painted.
8 It has become more popular / more multi-cultural. / More people have moved there. / ...

A presentation about William Shakespeare

1b) but you can still see his plays in many theatres today.
2c) had two daughters and a son.
3 His son died when he was only eleven years old.
4a) hotels.
5a) You couldn't sit down. / People had to stand. / ...
b) Female roles were played by men. / There were no female actors / no women on stage. / Men played female parts. / ...
6 **1 B · 2 D · 3 A**
7 They are made of wood. · They have low ceilings. · They have small windows.
8b) is a modern copy of the theatre from Shakespeare's days.

MUSTERPRÜFUNG 1: Leseverstehen ▶ S. 41–43

High-rise living in Britain

1c) often in poor condition.
2 false ... *because the text says* ... that in several cities, councils destroyed some of their high-rise apartment blocks. / ...
3 see lots of things. / enjoy the view from their flat. / ...
4 true ... *because the text says* ... that people in tower blocks often say that they feel safer than in a house. / that nobody can climb through the window of a flat on the 16th floor. / ...
5b) there aren't any insects or other small animals living in them.
6 Houses are too expensive. · People don't have time for garden work. · Houses can be broken into more easily. · You get more ants, mice and spiders in houses than in tower blocks.
7c) the way into the building is not dangerous.
8 false ... *because the text says* ... that this is often less costly than traditional building techniques. / ...
9 false ... *because the text says* ... that it's often easier to get to know your neighbours by chatting over the garden fence than by sharing the lift. / ...
10b) helps against heart disease.
11 true ... *because the text says* ... that if we want to protect our countryside, we will have to build them in our cities. / ...

MUSTERPRÜFUNG 1: Wortschatz ▶ S. 44–45

The joys of travelling

1 deal/cope · *2* missed · *3* relax / hang out / stay / chill / lie / sun-bathe / lounge · *4* kind/sort/type · *5a)* annoyed · *6* solve · *7c)* adventures. · *8* forget · *9d)* way. · *10c)* instead · *11d)* fixing · *12* strangers · *13b)* appreciate

MUSTERPRÜFUNG 1: Schreiben ▶ S. 46–47

Hinweis zu den Lösungsvorschlägen beim Schreiben:
- Teilaufgaben 1 (Textverständnis) und 2 (Textinterpretation) stützen sich stark auf den zugrunde liegenden Lesetext. Für diese Teilaufgaben werden daher englischsprachige Lösungsbeispiele angeboten. Sie sind als Orientierungshilfe gedacht. Es sind aber auch andere (inhaltlich ähnliche) Lösungen denkbar.
- Teilaufgaben 3a (argumentatives Schreiben) und 3b (kreatives Schreiben) sind freier angelegt. Dadurch gibt es eine noch größere Bandbreite an möglichen (auch inhaltlich sehr unterschiedlichen) Lösungen. Für diese Teilaufgaben wird daher auf Deutsch skizziert, welche Aspekte dein Text beinhalten sollte.
- Inhalt und Struktur deines Textes sind wichtig, aber Sprache und Ausdruck fließen noch stärker in die Benotung ein. Achte daher auf die Hinweise zur Bewertung von Ausdruck und Sprache auf S. 30.

My first journey abroad

1. Aufgabe zur Sicherung des Textverständnisses
Lösungsbeispiel:

Paul is an English teenager. He had German and French at school, but he found these languages very difficult to learn. The result was that he was scared of travelling to a country where people speak a different language than him.
And this is why he first said "No" when his friend Phil suggested a holiday abroad. But Phil really wanted to go cycling in France, and in the end Paul agreed to go with him. They earned the money for the trip by working in a cafe.

2. Aufgabe zur grundlegenden Interpretation
Lösungsbeispiel:

In Calais, Paul first felt more confident when Phil asked for directions and a woman answered in English. But he got nervous again in the hostel because he and Phil had to share a room with two Serbs who couldn't speak English.
Luckily, however, the Serbs were very friendly, and they tried to communicate with Paul and Phil. When they found out that one of the Serbs was also called Filip, they cheered and shared a bar of chocolate. Then they tried to say something more complicated. It took a long time, and the Serbs used drawings and acted things out – but again they managed to communicate, and this time they shared their food and the boys all ate together.
This experience in Calais was so important for Paul because he learned to be less frightened about being with people who don't speak his language. He learned that you can make friends even if you can't say a lot.

3a) Argumentatives Schreiben
Du beginnst deine **persönliche Stellungnahme** mit einer kurzen zum Thema **hinführenden Einleitung**.
Im Mittelteil gibst du **Argumente für und gegen die Aussage** wieder und wägst sie gegeneinander ab (z. B. bereichernde Qualität des direkten Austauschs mit anderen Kulturen, Gefühl von Sicherheit in der eigenen Heimat, finanzielle Überlegungen usw.). Du stützt deine Argumentation mit **eigenen Erfahrungen** auf Auslandsreisen, bei Begegnungen mit Menschen unterschiedlicher Herkunft in der eigenen Stadt oder mit Fernsehsendungen, aus denen du etwas über die Welt erfahren hast, und formulierst auf dieser Basis deine **persönliche Meinung** zu der Aussage.
Zum Schluss formulierst du ein **Fazit**, das sich nachvollziehbar und plausibel aus deinen Ausführungen ergibt.

3b) Kreatives Schreiben
Du entwickelst die Geschichte weiter, indem du die **Situation** von Phil und Paul aufgreifst und die Ereignisse des nächsten Tages unter **Berücksichtigung der Umstände** (Ort, Zeit) plausibel schilderst.
Du stellst **mögliche weitere Schwierigkeiten** dar, denen sich Paul stellen muss.
Du führst **mögliche Lösungsversuche** zu den Schwierigkeiten, die er erlebt, auf.
Du formulierst eine **Zusammenfassung** zu Pauls möglicherweise veränderten Haltung zu Fremden und Fremdsprachen.

> MUSTERPRÜFUNG 2: Hörverstehen ▶ S. 48–50

A True Short Story

1b) *and a few weekends during term time.*
2 *He wasn't available to work every day. / Tom couldn't work every day. / He was still too busy with school. / He had no work experience. / He had never had a job before. / …*

3c) *Tom applied for jobs.* · *4b)* *was unable to think of something to say.* · *5* *false* · *6c)* *worried.* · *7a)* *she had been too busy.*
8a) *Tom is polite and patient with customers. / Tom is very friendly with customers. / …*
b) *Tom gets on well with his colleagues. / Tom is friendly with his colleagues. / Tom has a good relationship with his colleagues. / …*

Cricket in India

1c) *have the most fans in the world.*
2c) *a little more than 50 % of all the people in the world are football fans.*
3a) *fell between 2007 and 2015.*
4c) *is almost as successful as Australia in world cricket.*
5b) *is the country where cricket was born.*
6a) *are Indian and play in India.*
7 *The money in cricket comes from advertising. / There is a lot of advertising involved. / Companies pay a lot of money to advertise their products at cricket games. / Rich people go to cricket games, so they are a great place for companies to advertise their products. / …*
8a) *think that cricket is not really a sport.*
9 *A new type of cricket called Twenty20 was invented with shorter, more exciting games.* · *Women's cricket has become more popular.*

> MUSTERPRÜFUNG 2: Leseverstehen ▶ S. 51–53

Life in South Africa today

1c) *more than in most countries.*
2 *true … because the text says … that under apartheid "black people could not vote".*
3 *false … because the text says … that "the country has eleven official languages".*
4 *The country celebrates its multicultural society.* · *South Africa has eleven official languages.* · *All South Africans enjoy equal rights.*
5 *true … because the text says … that "changes for the better are coming too slowly for many black South Africans".*
6b) *about half of black South Africans are poor.*
7a) *Schools with mostly black students are not as well equipped (too few computers and toilets) as schools with mostly white students. / Schools in mostly black areas have poorer facilities. / …*
b) *It's difficult to find teachers who can speak one of the official African languages. / Teachers who can speak one of the nine official African languages are often hard to find. / …*
8 *Many children whose parents have died from HIV have to manage their own lives.* · *If their parents die, they have to leave school in order to look after younger brothers and sisters.* · *They are scared of falling ill themselves.*
9a) *had more money to spend than it did later.*
10 *B, C*
11 *false … because the text says … that "there is little real mixing of the two different populations".*

> MUSTERPRÜFUNG 2: Wortschatz ▶ S. 54–55

How shopping has changed

1 *husband* · *2* *meat/things* · *3d)* *served* · *4* *queue/line/row* · *5a)* *basket* · *6c)* *carry* · *7* *environment/planet/world/earth* · *8* *instead* · *9d)* *High* · *10* *escalators* · *11c)* *growth* · *12c)* *search* · *13* *result/consequence/effect/drawback/downside/advantage/disadvantage*

MUSTERPRÜFUNG 2: Schreiben ▶ S. 56–57

1. Aufgabe zur Sicherung des Textverständnisses
Lösungsbeispiel:

Young people often fight with their parents. For example, they often want to stay out late at night, get more pocket money, or work at weekends to earn some money. Unlike their parents, teenagers don't always care for eating meals with the family at a dining table.

But the biggest difference between the two generations today is the use of technology and the social media: many young people like to watch films on their smartphones, and not together with their parents on the family TV set. They use social media to communicate with their friends, whereas their parents are used to talking on the phone or meeting their friends. And while the older generation prefers to read print newspapers, young people today get their news from the internet. This sometimes means that young people want to talk about things (e.g. video clips that have gone viral) that their parents aren't interested in.

2. Aufgabe zur grundlegenden Interpretation
Lösungsbeispiel:

According to Jacob, there are three main reasons for the differences between the generations:

First, there are arguments about trust and independence. For example, Jacob understands that young people often want to have their parents' trust and become more independent. So when their parents ask them to be home by a certain time, young people often feel insulted because they think that their parents don't trust them.

Next, the two generations have different attitudes. One example Jacob mentions is about different dinner habits: members of the older generation grew up at a time when it was normal to eat dinner at a table with the whole family. So when their children refuse to do this, parents will think that they are being antisocial. And finally, technology has changed quickly, so the two generations have completely different ways of using technology. Jacob thinks that people from the older generation don't use social media and the internet very much because they aren't used to them or because they worry about the dangers that they might bring. So while many parents stick to their old ways of communicating and dealing with the world, their children grew up with the internet and use it all the time.

Jacob is certain that these differences are normal. Every family will go through times when the younger and older members don't agree about some things. But this is often just a phase and these differences will become less important with time.

3a) Argumentatives Schreiben
Du beginnst deine **persönliche Stellungnahme** mit einer kurzen zum Thema **hinführenden Einleitung**.

Im **Mittelteil** beschreibst kurz deine **eigene Erfahrung** bezüglich Lebensstil (z. B. Regeln, Benehmen, Umgang mit Technologie).
Du **kommentierst** die Aussage unter Bezugnahme auf deine **persönliche Meinung** (z. B. Verständnis für die Sorge von Eltern, Gründe für eigene Meinungen, Verständnis dafür, dass Benehmen unterschiedlich interpretiert werden kann).
Du führst außerdem **konkrete Beispiele** für Situationen auf, in denen andere Lebensstile und Meinungen eine wesentliche Rolle gespielt haben.
Am Ende formulierst du auf der Basis deiner Ausführungen ein **Fazit**, das diese Unterschiede zwischen den Generationen als positiv oder negativ bewertet. Diese Schlussfolgerung sollte sich nachvollziehbar und plausibel aus deinen Ausführungen ergeben.

3b) Kreatives Schreiben
Du entwickelst das Gespräch, indem du die **Situation** von Katie und ihren Eltern aufgreifst und unter Berücksichtigung der Umstände (Ort, Zeit) plausibel weiterführst.
Du gibst Katies **Meinung und Argumente** wieder.
Du führst **mögliche Reaktionen** von Katies Eltern zu den Meinungen und Argumenten ihrer Tochter auf und gibst eigene Meinungen und Argumente der Eltern wieder.
Du führst **mögliche Reaktionen** von Katie zu den Meinungen und Argumenten ihrer Eltern auf.
Du bringst das Gespräch zu einem **plausiblen Schluss**. Dies kann eine Einigung, eine Zusammenfassung der Differenzen, eine Vertagung des Gesprächs oder ein Scheitern sein.

MUSTERPRÜFUNG 3: Hörverstehen ▶ S. 58–60

The D of E expedition

1 *true*
2 *B, C, E*
3 *three months volunteering · three months doing a new sport or physical activity · three months practising a special skill · a two-day expedition*
4 *c) and more volunteering, sport and skill work.*
5 *The four friends didn't lose their way. · The weather was good. · They kept up a good speed. · The tent didn't fall down.*
6 *b) the ground was hard.*
7 *A, C, D, E*
8 *She is worrying that she might not have the strength to continue. / that she might have to drop out. / that she will have to let the others carry on without her. / …*

A presentation about Wales

1 *b) Wales reached the semi-finals. · 2 true · 3 c) not like English at all.*
4 *west coast of Ireland · some parts of Brittany · north-west of France*
5 *the north and west of Wales*
6 *a) lots of farm animals.*
7 *b) were built by an English king to help him rule the people of Wales.*
8 *a) Coal was exported from Wales to Australia.*
b) So many Welsh people have emigrated to Australia that a state there is called New South Wales.

MUSTERPRÜFUNG 3: Leseverstehen ▶ S. 61–63

Good health in Australia?

1 *c) the fewest medals since 1992.*
2 *the populations of the different countries. / how many people live in the those countries. / medals per head of population.*
3 *false … because the text says … that they are volunteers.*
4 *true … because the text says … that one of their jobs is to deal with thieves on the beach.*
5 *b) give a positive picture of Australia.*
6 *false … because the text says … that two out of three Australians are overweight or obese. / that two thirds of all Australians are overweight or obese. / …*
7 *a) Overweight is bad for peoples' health. / increases the risk of diseases like diabetes and cancer. / can cause heart diseases as well as Type 2 diabetes or cancer. / …*
b) Overweight increases the nationwide cost of medical treatment. / raises public spending on healthcare. / forces Australia to spend more money on treating obese or overweight patients. / …

8 c) only a small minority of Australians eat enough vegetables.
9 true … because the text says … that these figures exclude those over 64 years of age / older than 64. / …
10 b) have not gone down anywhere in the world.
11 true … because the text says … that holiday brochures and TV series only show slim and healthy Australians. / that the rise in obesity rates contrasts starkly with Australia's self-image of fitness and health. / …

MUSTERPRÜFUNG 3: Wortschatz ▶ S. 64–65

Life in the Outback

1 population · 2 c) comparable · 3 building/block/tower · 4 even/any/real/many · 5 a) impassable · 6 d) advance · 7 hand · 8 b) cattle. · 9 problems/difficulties/issues · 10 d) education. · 11 little · 12 forward · 13 b) relationships

MUSTERPRÜFUNG 3: Schreiben ▶ S. 66–67

1. Aufgabe zur Sicherung des Textverständnisses
Lösungsbeispiel:

Morwenna has a brother and a sister – and very strict parents. There have always been rules that she and her siblings had to follow. For example, they had to wash their hands, eat whatever they got, tidy up their rooms, and be polite.
Now that Morwenna is older, there are new rules too. For example, she has to text her parents every hour when she's out of the house. She isn't allowed to stay out later than nine o'clock in the evening unless she's going to the theatre. Visits to the cinema have to be in the afternoon or early evening, and her parents always want to know the name of the film.
Since she is never home late, Morwenna spends most evenings together with her family. They talk about things and have a real family life. That's important to her.
And although Morwenna's parents are stricter than most parents, they never use force. So all things considered, Morwenna is happy with her home life.

2. Aufgabe zur grundlegenden Interpretation
Lösungsbeispiel:

Morwenna admits that her parents were (and still are) strict. On the one hand, she has not always been happy with their rules. She thinks that sometimes her parents exaggerated, like when she was not allowed to watch a Harry Potter film together with her friends. So at times she has been jealous of the freedom that her friends enjoyed, for example the freedom to come home later in the evenings.
But on the other hand, Morwenna thinks that her parents' rules have been good for her. Thanks to her parents' rules Morwenna has good teeth, eats a great variety of foods and is able to take good care of her things – so she feels more independent and grown-up. And unlike some of her friends who fight with their parents a lot, Morwenna has a real family life, and she is proud of it.
On the whole, Morwenna feels that although her parents are strict, they have always loved her and cared about her well-being and safety. She thinks that their rules have helped her grow up.

3a) Argumentatives Schreiben
Du beginnst deine **persönliche Stellungnahme** mit einer kurzen zum Thema **hinführenden Einleitung**.
Im **Mittelteil** wägst du **Argumente für** (z. B. Freunde verstehen dich besser, Eltern haben wenig Zeit, Lehrer haben kein Interesse für persönliche Lebensfragen) **und gegen das Statement** (z. B. Freunde sind selbst unerfahren, Eltern wollen dein Bestes,

Lehrer sind neutral) gegeneinander ab.
Bist du für das Statement, so beginnst du mit den Argumenten dagegen. Bist du gegen das Statement, so beginnst du mit den Argumenten dafür.
Du stützt deine Argumente durch **konkrete Beispiele** (z. B. eigene Erfahrungen in Bezug auf den Einfluss von Eltern, Lehrern und Freunden).
Abschließend formulierst du auf der Basis deiner Ausführungen ein **Fazit**, das sich nachvollziehbar und plausibel aus deinen Ausführungen ergibt.

3b) Kreatives Schreiben
Du beginnst deinen **Leserbrief** mit der Anrede *(Dear Sir or Madam / Dear Editor)* und nennst den Anlass deines Schreibens (Reaktion auf Morwennas Artikel).
Im **Mittelteil** äußerst du deine **Meinung** über Morwennas Artikel (Zustimmung oder Ablehnung). Du greifst Aspekte ihres Artikels auf und unterstützt sie oder widersprichst ihr durch eigene Argumente, Erfahrungen und Beispiele, wobei dein wichtigstes Argument oder Gegenargument zum Schluss kommt. Dabei verwendest du eine sachliche, klare Sprache.
Zum Schluss fasst du deine Meinung zusammen, verdeutlichst sie und ziehst daraus ein nachvollziehbares **Fazit** zum Thema elterliche Regeln. Du grüßt *(Yours faithfully / Yours sincerely / Best regards / …)* und unterschreibst mit deinem eigenen Namen.

Notentabelle

Punkte	Note
104–120	sehr gut
88–103	gut
71–87	befriedigend
54–70	ausreichend
22–53	mangelhaft
0–21	ungenügend

ABSCHLUSS-PRÜFUNGS-TRAINER

Nordrhein-Westfalen

Musterprüfungen

Erster Prüfungsteil: Hörverstehen – Leseverstehen

1. Hörverstehen – Teil 1

Bo-Kaap – a special district in Cape Town

A tourist guide is giving a tour of the Bo-Kaap district in Cape Town, South Africa.

> - *First read the tasks (1–8).*
> - *Then listen to the guide.*
> - *While you are listening, tick the correct box, answer the question or fill in the information.*
> - *At the end you will hear the guide again.*
> - *Now read the tasks (1–8). You have **90 seconds** to do this.*

🎧 **10**
> - *Now listen to the guide and do the tasks.*

1 The Bo-Kaap mosque was built ...

   a) ☐ at the end of the 18th century.

   b) ☐ a hundred years ago.

   c) ☐ in 1974.

2 Back then, Cape Town was governed by Europeans.

   This statement is ...   ☐ true   ☐ false

3 The people from India and South-East Asia had a hard life in South Africa. Give **one** example.

   _____

4 Over one million people in South Africa ...

   a) ☐ are Muslim.

   b) ☐ are Asian.

   c) ☐ are from Bo-Kaap.

5 What sort of work did Asian workers do outside of Cape Town?

   a) _____

   b) _____

6 The Bo-Kaap Museum ...

   a) ☐ was built in 1964.

   b) ☐ has exhibitions but no furniture.

   c) ☐ gives information about the Asian population of Cape Town.

7 The special thing in this part of Wale Street is ...

a) ☐ the language of the people who live there.

b) ☐ that the houses are brightly painted.

c) ☐ that there are many different shops.

8 How has Bo-Kaap changed in the last few years? Give **one** example.

_____

_____

A street in Bo-Kaap

2. Hörverstehen – Teil 2

A presentation about William Shakespeare

Amina and Mason are giving a presentation about William Shakespeare.

- *First read the tasks (1–8).*
- *Then listen to the presentation.*
- *While you are listening, tick the correct box, answer the question, match the sentence halves or fill in the information.*
- *At the end you will hear the presentation again.*
- *Now read the tasks (1–8). You have **90 seconds** to do this.*

🎧
11

- *Now listen to the presentation and do the tasks.*

1 Shakespeare wrote his plays many years ago, ...

a) ☐ so his plays are mostly read, but not performed today.

b) ☐ but you can still see his plays in many theatres today.

c) ☐ so today you can only see them in Britain.

2 Not much is known about Shakespeare's private life. But we know that he ...

a) ☐ was born and died in London.

b) ☐ married at the age of 20.

c) ☐ had two daughters and a son.

William Shakespeare (1564–1616)

3 William Shakespeare suffered a tragedy in his family. What happened?

_____

4 The inns where William Shakespeare put on his plays were a bit like ...

a) ☐ hotels.

b) ☐ schools.

c) ☐ churches.

5 Putting on plays was different in Shakespeare's time. Name **two** differences.

a) _____

b) _____

6 Match the place names (1–3) with the explanations (A–E). You won't need **two** letters.

		A	is the place where Shakespeare went to school.
1	The house in Henley Street ...	**B**	is the place where Shakespeare was born.
2	Mary Arden's house ...	**C**	is the place where Shakespeare's father worked.
3	Old Town Hall ...	**D**	is the place owned by Shakespeare's mother.
		E	is the place where Shakespeare met his wife.

7 What is special about the old buildings from Shakespeare's time? Give **two** examples.

– _____

– _____

8 The Globe Theatre in London today ...

a) ☐ is the same old theatre in which Shakespeare put on his plays.

b) ☐ is a modern copy of the theatre from Shakespeare's days.

c) ☐ is completely different from the sort of theatre that Shakespeare used.

3. Leseverstehen

High-rise living in Britain

The following text is from the lifestyle section of a British newspaper.

High-rise apartment blocks have long had a bad press in Britain. People think of the 1960s tower blocks that were usually built for people in lower-paid jobs. The flats were small and the
5 entrances were dark and dirty, full of litter and graffiti. The lifts kept breaking down. That was no joke if you lived on the 10th floor and arrived home with your week's shopping or a child in a wheelchair. The general view was that people
10 only lived in such buildings if they had no alternative. In several cities, councils destroyed some of their high-rise apartment blocks.

Of course, the tower blocks have always had their fans, above all because of the amazing
15 views that residents often have from their flats. In addition, people in tower blocks often say that they feel safer than in a house. That's because nobody can climb through the window of a flat on the 16th floor: in fact, nobody can even
20 look in, so you don't have to draw your curtains at night. And the flats are largely free from mice, ants and spiders. These voices, however, were long in the minority. Not any more.

Look at the skyline of most British cities
25 today and you'll see that apartment blocks are going up all around you. Why this sudden popularity of flats? One reason is that with land becoming more and more expensive, houses are simply costing too much for many people. Build-
30 ing taller, it seems, is the only way of building cheaper homes. And the new trend for flats also reflects a change in lifestyle. In the past, a house with a garden was seen as an ideal, but these days many people get home late from work – so
35 they have no time for garden work. Instead, they prefer to have a few plants on an easily-managed balcony.

What's more, the apartments that have been built in the last few years attract people on
40 good incomes. They are large and airy. CCTV cameras keep the entrances safe, and companies are employed to clean the corridors and maintain the lifts. Some of these modern flats are built as 'pods' – that is to say, each flat is built
45 as a self-contained unit, with bathrooms and kitchen equipped to a high standard, and the pods are then simply placed one on top of the

Tower block in London

other. This is often less costly than traditional building techniques, and customers can make their choice of equipment as they would do if
50 they were buying a car.

It is true that families with children still usually prefer to live in a house with a front door, a back door and a garden. Parents can keep an eye on their children, and it's often easier to
55 get to know your neighbours by chatting over the garden fence than by sharing the lift up the 8th floor. But a recent report has challenged the widely-held view that high-rise blocks offer a less healthy environment.
60

Experts from the University of Bern in Switzerland found that people who live on the 8th floor or above are likely to live longer than those who live on the lower floors. Those living higher up, they claim, are 40 % less likely to die of lung
65 disease, and 35 % less likely to die from heart disease – partly because walking up more stairs keeps people fitter. There is also less air pollution on the higher floors and people are also less affected by traffic noise.
70

The British population is expected to grow from about 65 million in 2016 to 75 million by 2040, so millions of new homes will have to be built. If we want to protect our countryside, we will have to build them in our cities, and as the
75 price of land in cities goes up, it is clear that more people will have to live in flats. The apartment blocks being built today are here to stay.

- *First read the text.*
- *Then do the tasks (1–11).*
- *For tasks 1, 5, 7 and 10 tick the correct box.*
- *For tasks 2, 4, 8, 9 and 11 decide if the statements are true or false and tick the correct box. Then finish these sentences. You can quote from the text.*
- *For tasks 3 and 6 fill in the information.*

---

1 The flats in the 1960s tower blocks were …

    a) ☐ not always clean, but at least had good lifts instead of stairs.

    b) ☐ ideal for families with disabled children.

    c) ☐ often in poor condition.

2 No 1960s tower blocks exist today because all British cities have taken them down.

    This statement is …   ☐ true   ☐ false   … because the text says …

    _____

3 What people like most about living in high-rise buildings is that they can …

    _____

4 Some people don't want to live in houses because they're afraid of people breaking into their homes.

    This statement is …   ☐ true   ☐ false   … because the text says …

    _____

5 One advantage of flats described in the text is that …

    a) ☐ they are very bright.

    b) ☐ there aren't any insects or other small animals living in them.

    c) ☐ the walls are thicker, so you don't hear the neighbours.

6 More people see some disadvantages with living in houses. Give **two** downsides.

    – _____

    – _____

7 In many of the most recent apartment buildings ...

a) ☐ the flats are quite small.

b) ☐ the heating systems are very efficient.

c) ☐ the way into the building is not dangerous.

8 Building with 'pods' gives people more choice, but it's more expensive than other ways of building.

This statement is ... ☐ true ☐ false ... because the text says ...

_____

9 People who live in flats are more likely to make friends with their neighbours than people who live in houses.

This statement is ... ☐ true ☐ false ... because the text says ...

_____

10 Living on higher floors in apartment blocks ...

a) ☐ is louder.

b) ☐ helps against heart disease.

c) ☐ is dangerous because the air is dirtier.

11 The writer is concerned about the fields and rivers around the cities.

This statement is ... ☐ true ☐ false ... because the text says ...

_____

Zweiter Prüfungsteil: Wortschatz – Schreiben

4. Wortschatz

The joys of travelling

Yolanda from Poland loves travelling. She gives some of her reasons in an article for an online magazine.

> • *Fill in suitable words or tick the correct box.*

I really think that travelling helps people to become better persons. I'll tell you why.

1 Travelling helps you to be more flexible and confident because you learn to _____

with unexpected problems.

2 You may, for example, have to decide what to do if you arrive at the station and find out that you

have _____ your train.

3 Or you may have to make alternative plans if you wanted to be lazy and _____

on the beach all day, but you can't because it's raining.

4 Of course, this _____ of situation is really irritating.

5 Your first reaction is to feel …
a) ☐ annoyed **b)** ☐ sensible **c)** ☐ shy **d)** ☐ excited
because you can't do what you wanted to do.

6 But so often when you travel you meet people who can help you _____ your problem.

You start chatting, you share a joke, and you feel much better.

7 After this has happened a few times, you realize that such difficulties aren't really problems because
they lead to new, positive experiences and …
a) ☐ complications. **b)** ☐ exercises. **c)** ☐ adventures. **d)** ☐ troubles.
In fact, this is how you make many new friends.

8 And of course lots of these challenging moments make wonderful stories to share with your friends

when you get home. Keep a diary, so that you don't _____ these moments!

9 Another good thing about travelling is that you learn things about other countries in a very enjoyable ...

a) ☐ history. b) ☐ culture. c) ☐ part. d) ☐ way.

10 You really experience other cultures, other foods, other lifestyles ...

a) ☐ apart b) ☐ unless c) ☐ instead d) ☐ because

of only reading about them in boring old books.

11 And maybe you'll pick up new skills like cooking new foods, reading maps and ...

a) ☐ getting b) ☐ buying c) ☐ throwing d) ☐ fixing

things when they break — because you can't buy replacements easily.

12 And you'll certainly pick up the best skill of all: the ability to trust total _____

— people who you have never met before.

13 And finally, it's when you're far away from home that you'll probably really ...

a) ☐ improve b) ☐ appreciate c) ☐ hate d) ☐ influence

your home and your parents as you never have before. That will make it easier for you when you

return home at the end of your journey.

Yolanda

5. Schreiben

My first journey abroad

Paul, an English teenager, writes about a fantastic experience during his first journey abroad.

I was never any good at foreign languages at school. German was our first foreign language, and I could never understand why they had so many different words that all meant *the*.
5   When I wrote *der* the teacher said it should be *den*, or *die* or *dem* – but I never understood why. Then in Year 8 we had French as our second foreign language, and that was even harder. I didn't learn much, I never enjoyed the lessons,
10 and my marks were awful.

My sad experience of learning languages made me nervous about travelling abroad. How, I thought, could I tell a hotel receptionist that I needed a toothbrush? Or how could I even find
15 the way to the hotel if all the signs were in a language that I couldn't understand? It seemed like a nightmare.

So when Phil, my best friend at school, suggested a cycling holiday in France, I first said
20 "No". But he kept trying to persuade me because he really didn't want to go alone. So in the end I said "OK, I'll go!"

So in mid-August, after we had both worked in a fast-food cafe for a month to earn some
25 money, we travelled down to Dover and put our bikes on the ferry to France. I felt so nervous that my heart was beating fast.

In Calais we had to drive on the right, and soon we were lost because we couldn't under-
30 stand the signs. I didn't dare ask the way because I was scared that I wouldn't understand the answer. But then Phil stopped to ask a woman – and she answered in English! I began to feel better. If people in France could speak
35 English, I had nothing to be afraid of …

Imagine my disappointment, then, when we arrived at our hostel in Calais and found that we were sharing a four-bed dormitory with two guys from Serbia who spoke no English at all.
40 "This will be a very quiet evening," I thought.

But then one of the guys came over and said something, pointed at Phil and smiled. Then he said it again. I tried to explain that I couldn't understand Serbian, but he just smiled.
45 He pointed at himself and said "Filip". And then he pointed at Phil and said the same word again – and I suddenly realized what he meant.

Philip & Filip

"Ah, you're both called Philip," I said. "He Philip," I added and pointed at Phil, "and you Filip," pointing at him. And he cheered. I felt 50 better. Then Filip pointed at his friend and said "Dragan". He took out a bar of chocolate and shared it with us.

Then Filip said something else, something much longer. I tried to recognize some words, 55 but I couldn't. Filip took out a pen and drew something on a piece of paper. Was it a cushion? No, he drew a head under it. Was it a hat? If so, it was a strange hat. Then he drew the Union Jack. And a woman. And a big building – it looked like 60 a palace.

And suddenly I shouted "The Queen! Elizabeth!" Filip nodded and laughed and we gave each other five. And so it went on with words, and drawings, and acting things out. And finally 65 we understood what he wanted to say: Filip and Dragan had been to London and they had seen the Queen. When we got the whole sentence, we all cheered. Then Dragan took out some bread and sausage and cheese from his bag and we all 70 ate together. We felt great.

It had taken us half an hour to understand Filip's sentence – and it wasn't a very important sentence. But that didn't matter. He had communicated, we had understood, and that had 75 brought us closer together. And suddenly I felt less nervous about our trip.

However, the next day, after we had said goodbye to Filip and Dragan, …

1 *Describe what you know about Paul before he left England.*

2 *Explain what happened in Calais and why it is so important for Paul.*

3 *You have a choice here. Choose one of the following tasks.*

a) *"You don't have to travel: you can meet the world on TV or in your home town."*

Comment on the statement from your point of view.

Include the following aspects:
- *Give reasons in favour of and against this statement.*
- *Give examples from your experience.*
- *Give your personal opinion on the statement.*
- *Write a conclusion and state what you think about travelling or staying at home.*

or

b) *"However, the next day, after we had said goodbye to Filip and Dragan, ..."*

Write a suitable ending in the way the story is told.

Include the following aspects:
- *Continue Paul's description of the holiday.*
- *Describe the next day's adventure:*
  - *a problem that they faced*
  - *how they found a solution*
  - *how this made Paul feel better about travelling abroad.*

Erster Prüfungsteil: Hörverstehen – Leseverstehen

1. Hörverstehen – Teil 1

A True Short Story

The daily *Kathy Foster Morning Radio Show* includes a series called *A True Short Story*. Today's story is about Tom and his very first job.

> - *First read the tasks (1–8).*
> - *Then listen to the story.*
> - *While you are listening, tick the correct box, fill in the information or answer the questions.*
> - *At the end you will hear the story again.*
> - *Now read the tasks. You have **90 seconds** to do this.*

🎧
12

> - *Now listen to the story and do the tasks.*

1 Tom wanted a job. He could work in the school holidays …

   a) ☐ and at weekends during term time.

   b) ☐ and a few weekends during term time.

   c) ☐ but not during term time.

2 Employers didn't want to give Tom a job. Give **one** reason why.

_____

3 At the jobs fair …

   a) ☐ Tom didn't manage to talk to many employers.

   b) ☐ people weren't nice to Tom.

   c) ☐ Tom applied for jobs.

4 When Linda offered Tom some work, Tom …

   a) ☐ asked how much he would earn.

   b) ☐ was unable to think of something to say.

   c) ☐ was disappointed because the pay was bad.

5 Tom did different kinds of tasks, but he was not allowed to prepare meals.

   This statement is … ☐ true ☐ false

6 When Tom was at work and thought of Linda, he felt …

   a) ☐ very confident.

   b) ☐ a bit bored.

   c) ☐ worried.

7 Linda told Tom that she hadn't talked with him much because ...

a) ☐ she had been too busy.

b) ☐ managers should not talk too much with their workers.

c) ☐ she had been away.

8 What did Linda say about Tom's relationship with customers and colleagues?

a) _____

b) _____

2. Hörverstehen – Teil 2

Cricket in India

Aarav Malhotra is a radio reporter in Delhi. You are going to hear a radio interview about the sport cricket and the role of India for the sport.

> • *First read the tasks (1–9).*
> • *Then listen to the interview.*
> • *While you are listening, tick the correct box, fill in the information or answer the questions.*
> • *At the end you will hear the interview again.*
> • *Now read the tasks. You have **90 seconds** to do this.*

🎧 13

> • *Now listen to the interview and do the tasks.*

1 Aarav Malhotra's question is which two sports ...

a) ☐ have the most players in the word.

b) ☐ are played in most countries in the world.

c) ☐ have the most fans in the world.

2 If we don't count young children, then ...

a) ☐ a large majority of all the people in the world are football fans.

b) ☐ almost 50 % of all the people in the world are football fans.

c) ☐ a little more than 50 % of all the people in the world are football fans.

3 The number of countries in the Cricket World Cup ...

a) ☐ fell between 2007 and 2015.

b) ☐ has risen with every tournament.

c) ☐ is bigger than in the Basketball World Cup.

India's Rohit Sharma during the ICC Champions Trophy in Cardiff, Wales (2013)

4 India ...

a) ☐ has won the Cricket World Cup more often than any other country.

b) ☐ is more successful than Australia in world cricket.

c) ☐ is almost as successful as Australia in world cricket.

5 England ...

a) ☐ has won the Cricket World Cup twice.

b) ☐ is the country where cricket was born.

c) ☐ is more successful at international cricket than India.

6 The cricket players who earn the most money ...

a) ☐ are Indian and play in India.

b) ☐ are Europeans and Americans who play in India.

c) ☐ were once Indian, but not any more.

7 Why is there money in Indian cricket?

_____

8 According to Aarav, people in countries that don't play cricket ...

a) ☐ think that cricket is not really a sport.

b) ☐ think that cricket is a modern sport.

c) ☐ are familiar with the rules of the game.

9 Cricket has changed in the last few years. Give **one** example of how it has changed.

_____

3. Leseverstehen

Life in South Africa today

This is an online magazine article about life for young South Africans today.

In all countries society is constantly changing, but few countries have changed as radically as South Africa. Before the country's first free elections in 1994, everything in your life depended on the colour of your skin. Under a system called *apartheid*, black and white people lived in different zones, went to different schools, had different jobs, relaxed on different beaches and even used different public toilets. Black people could not vote, and marriages between black and white people were forbidden. This system led to street protests by the black population, which were violently put down by the forces of the white government. Many unarmed protesters were killed, many more were locked up in prison.

The election of Nelson Mandela, South Africa's first black president, in 1994 changed all that. *Apartheid* was abolished and all South Africans – black, white and Asian – now enjoy equal rights. The country has eleven official languages (English, Afrikaans and nine African languages), which means that local communities can send their children to schools which teach in their own language. South Africa has indeed been given the nickname of the *Rainbow Nation* because it celebrates its multicultural society.

But changes for the better are coming too slowly for many black South Africans who were born after 1994. The white population (nine percent of the total population) still has a larger proportion of the country's wealth than black South Africans, who make up 80 percent of the population. True, there is now a small number of black people who have also become rich, but about 54 percent of the black population live in poverty, according to a government report in 2014, compared to 0.8 percent of the white population.

You can see this inequality in many of South Africa's primary and secondary schools. Schools in mostly white areas of the country are well equipped, while many schools in mostly black areas have poor facilities – not only too few computers, but maybe only one toilet for 60 students. And schools that teach in one of the nine official African languages often find it difficult to employ teachers who can speak their language.

Life is particularly hard for girls because they suffer the most from violence in the streets. About one third of girls experience sexual violence before the age of 18. The rates of HIV infections are high, and over 60 percent of the victims are women. Many children have to manage life on their own because their parents die young, and they often have to leave school in order to look after younger brothers and sisters. The children are often terrified of falling ill themselves.

South Africa's economy is now growing by less than two percent a year, which is a lower increase than in the first years of the 21st century. This means that the government now has less money to spend on improving schools and social conditions.

South Africa's problems should not be exaggerated. The country has not been destroyed by violence. The economy is the biggest in Africa after Nigeria, and incomes per person are among the highest in Africa. Conditions have improved for most people, and blacks can now go onto beaches and into bars that were once reserved for whites. However, life is still hard for many South Africans. The gap between the standard of living of black and white South Africans is as large as ever, and there is little real mixing of the two different populations. So it's not surprising that more and more blacks are becoming impatient for real change.

> - *First read the text.*
> - *Then do the tasks 1 – 11.*
> - *For tasks 1, 6 and 9 tick the correct box.*
> - *For tasks 2, 3, 5 and 11 tick the correct box and quote from the text.*
> - *For tasks 4, 7 and 8 fill in the information.*
> - *For task 10 match the sentence beginning with the correct endings.*

1   The writer's opinion is that life in South Africa has changed ...

   a) ☐ less than in most countries.

   b) ☐ about the same as in most countries.

   c) ☐ more than in most countries.

2   Under *apartheid* black people were not allowed to take part in elections.

   This statement is ...   ☐ true   ☐ false   ... because the text says ...

   _____

3   English is the only official language of South Africa.

   This statement is ...   ☐ true   ☐ false   ... because the text says ...

   _____

4   Give **two** reasons why South Africa deserves the multicultural nickname of the *Rainbow Nation*.

   – _____

   – _____

5   Many black South Africans feel that conditions are not changing fast enough.

   This statement is ...   ☐ true   ☐ false   ... because the text says ...

   _____

6   The situation today, according to the text, is that ...

   a) ☐ all the rich people in South Africa are white.

   b) ☐ about half of black South Africans are poor.

   c) ☐ 80 % of black South Africans are very poor.

7   Many schools with mostly black students are still different from schools with mostly white students. Give **two** examples.

   a) _____

   b) _____

8 The high levels of HIV make life hard for many South African children. Give **two** examples.

– _____

– _____

9 In the first years of the 21st century the government ...

a) ☐ had more money to spend than it did later.

b) ☐ had less money to spend than it did later.

c) ☐ could spend less on schools than today.

10 Match the sentence beginning with the endings (A–E) to make true sentences.

South Africans today ...	**A** ... have the biggest economy in Africa. **B** ... earn more on average than people in most other African countries. **C** ... enjoy equal rights. **D** ... generally have the same lifestyle. **E** ... don't want their country to change.

11 Today there are lots of weddings between black and white partners in South Africa.

This statement is ...   ☐ true   ☐ false   ... because the text says ...

_____

Zweiter Prüfungsteil: Wortschatz – Schreiben

4. Wortschatz

How shopping has changed

Simon writes a blog that contrasts life for his great grandparents and himself. Read his blog about shopping.

> • *Fill in suitable words or tick the correct box.*

1 In my great grandparents' generation, it was

   the wife who went shopping while her

   _____ went to work.

   And in the evening she made his dinner for him.

2 At first, shopping meant going from shop to shop to buy different things. My great grandmother

   went to the baker's for bread, to the greengrocer's for fruit and vegetables, and to the butcher's for

   _____ like steak, ham and sausages.

3 My great grandmother said what she wanted, and each shopkeeper …
   a) ☐ supported **b)** ☐ suggested **c)** ☐ offered **d)** ☐ served
   her by picking the items off a shelf.

4 Of course, this all took a long time, so customers stood in a _____ and

   chatted with the people in front of them or behind them.

5 However, in the 1960s supermarkets began to appear, and my great grandmother got used to
   putting her groceries into a shopping …
   a) ☐ basket **b)** ☐ barn **c)** ☐ backpack **d)** ☐ baggage
   herself.

6 At the checkout she got lots of plastic bags to …
   a) ☐ lift **b)** ☐ pull **c)** ☐ carry **d)** ☐ wear
   her shopping home.

7 Back then nobody worried about what would happen to all those plastic bags. Nobody talked about

pollution and the problems this creates for our rivers, fields, animals and the sea – in fact the

problems for our whole _____ .

8 In the late 1970s, shopping changed again. Supermarkets got bigger and bigger, and customers like

my grandparents got used to paying by credit card _____ of cash.

9 And lots of shops moved away from the ...

a) ☐ Wide **b)** ☐ Head **c)** ☐ Large **d)** ☐ High

Street and out into shopping centres on the edge of town, where they had more space to expand.

10 The shopping experience was made as easy as possible. Outside, huge car parks appeared.

And inside the department stores, the stairs were replaced with lifts and _____

to whisk customers up to the upper floors.

11 Now that my parents' generation does most of the shopping, things are changing again. The most

recent development in the shopping experience is the rapid ...

a) ☐ return **b)** ☐ salary **c)** ☐ growth **d)** ☐ reverse

of online shopping.

12 Without even leaving their homes, customers simply ...

a) ☐ program **b)** ☐ buy **c)** ☐ search **d)** ☐ order

the supermarkets' websites, click on the items they require and pay online.

13 One _____ of online shopping is that some out-of-town shopping centres

are becoming smaller. There will certainly be other changes too, but it is still too early to predict

them.

5. Schreiben

Katie, a Scottish teenager, has written to the *Problems Page* of an online magazine.
Read her message and the magazine's answer.

I love my parents, but I find it more and more difficult to talk with them. We're interested in different things, and our lifestyles are different. My parents worry that I spend too much

5 time on my smartphone; I think it's normal. They think that the social media are dangerous; for me, the social media are part of my everyday life. And I find lots of their attitudes narrow and old-fashioned. I'm sure I'm not the only person

10 with this problem, but what can I do about it?
Katie

Hi Katie,

Thanks for your interesting message – and no, you are certainly not alone!

There are times in most families when the

5 younger members have little to say to the older members. And it's perfectly normal for young people to rebel against some of their parents' rules and attitudes.

Parents can become very angry if their kids

10 wish to stay out at night, or if they don't return by an agreed time. They argue with their kids about pocket money, about whether or not their kids should have a weekend job, about who should be responsible for choosing, buying and

15 washing their clothes ... and so the list goes on.

These arguments are, in essence, about trust and independence. But arguments can also be about attitudes. Your parents probably grew up at a time when families ate their meals

20 together at a dining table. They probably watched TV together because there was only one TV set per household. If you aren't interested in these things, parents often see this as a sign of laziness or antisocial behaviour – while you

25 may think it's perfectly normal.

These are problems that every generation has experienced (and in the end resolved), but your generation often feels even more different from their parents because technology has

30 moved on so quickly. You use your mobile to chat with your friends, but your parents probably still prefer to talk to their friends over the landline or face-to-face. You get your daily news on your smartphone while your parents prob-

35 ably get their daily news from print news-

papers or the TV because those are the sources that they trust. And while your parents may use the social media (e.g. to send photos), they probably spend less time on the social media than

40 you. This can be because the changes in technology come too fast for them or because they're afraid that they won't understand the technology. And of course many parents have read (sometimes exaggerated) stories about the po-

45 tential dangers of social media.

The developments in technology influence family life because maybe you use your phone while talking with your parents, or maybe you spend the evenings in your bedroom chatting

50 with your friends or watching videos. And this modern technology can influence your opinion about what is important in the world. A clip about a crime in, say, San Francisco may get tens of thousands of comments from people all

55 around the world, so in a sense we're becoming 'world citizens'. But your parents may be less concerned by some of these issues – so you have less to talk about.

But the most important point is this: you

60 write that you love your parents, and I'm sure your parents love you. That is more important than any of the points I have written about. It is perfectly normal for families to have times when there is less communication between

65 family members – but if you love each other, this will be a phase that will pass. You will soon look back on it and wonder why you took it so seriously.

Good luck!

Jacob Campbell (Problems Pages Team)

70

1 *Describe the differences between Katie's generation and her parents' generation according to the text.*

2 *Explain why – according to Jacob – the two different generations often have different opinions.*

3 *You have a choice here. Choose **one** of the following tasks.*

a) *"My parents' lifestyle and opinions are very different from mine."*

Comment on the statement from your point of view.

Include the following aspects:
* *Write about your own experience.*
* *Give your personal opinion on the statement. You can agree or disagree with it.*
* *Give examples of situations where your parents' lifestyle and opinions do or don't differ from yours.*
* *Write a conclusion and state whether having differences is good or bad.*

or

b) *Katie decides to talk about her problems with her parents.*

Imagine the conversation.

Include the following aspects:
* *Katie's words to her parents*
* *her parents' reactions to her points and some of their arguments*
* *Katie's reactions to her parents' arguments*
* *whether the conversation ends with understanding or in a quarrel*

Erster Prüfungsteil: Hörverstehen – Leseverstehen

1. Hörverstehen – Teil 1

The D of E expedition

You are going to hear an excerpt from *Summer Storms*, a book about a girl's adventurous summer in Britain. In this excerpt, Keira is on an expedition with her friends.

> • *First read the tasks (1–8).*
> • *Then listen to the story.*
> • *While you are listening, tick the correct box, say if the statements are true or false, answer the questions and fill in the information.*
> • *At the end you will hear the story again.*
> • *Now read the tasks (1–8). You have **90 seconds** to do this.*

🎧 **14** • *Now listen to the story and do the tasks.*

1 At the beginning of the story Keira just wants to relax.

This statement is ☐ true ☐ false

2 What does Keira tell us about the Duke of Edinburgh? Tick the correct statements.

Keira tells us that he ...

☐ **A** lives in Edinburgh.

☐ **B** is married to the Queen.

☐ **C** set up the *D of E Award* in 1956.

☐ **D** won first prize in a hiking competition.

☐ **E** wanted people to do exciting things in the outside world.

☐ **F** took part in the Olympic Games in 1956.

3 At bronze level, you have to face different challenges. Name **two** of them.

– _____

– _____

4 At silver level, compared with bronze, you do a longer hike ...

a) ☐ but the same amount of volunteering, sport and skill work.

b) ☐ but less volunteering, sport and skill work.

c) ☐ and more volunteering, sport and skill work.

5 The first day of hiking was no problem. Give **two** examples.

–

–

6 The problem during the first night was that ...

a) ☐ the tent fell down.

b) ☐ the ground was hard.

c) ☐ it rained into the tent.

7 What were the problems on the second day? Tick the correct sentences (A–F).

☐ **A** Their tents were wet.

☐ **B** They lost their map.

☐ **C** They lost their way.

☐ **D** They lost a shoe in the mud.

☐ **E** The hike took longer than expected.

☐ **F** They became very cold.

8 What is Keira worrying about on the morning of the third day?

2. Hörverstehen – Teil 2

A presentation about Wales

Four students in a school in Baltimore, USA, are giving a presentation about Wales.

- *First read the tasks (1–8).*
- *Then listen to the presentation.*
- *While you are listening, tick the correct box, say if the statements are true or false, answer the questions and fill in the information.*
- *At the end you will hear the presentation again.*
- *Now read the tasks (1–8). You have **90 seconds** to do this.*

- *Now listen to the presentation and do the tasks.*

1   In the EURO 2016 Football Championship ...

   a) ☐ Wales won against England.

   b) ☐ Wales reached the semi-finals.

   c) ☐ Wales did better than Germany.

2   Most people who live in Wales identify closely with Wales.

   This statement is ☐ true ☐ false

3   The Welsh language is ...

   a) ☐ a dialect of English.

   b) ☐ different from English, but with many similarities.

   c) ☐ not like English at all.

4   Dan mentions areas outside Wales where Celtic languages are spoken. Give **one** of his examples.

_____

5   The part of Wales in which you have the best chance of hearing people speaking Welsh is in

_____.

6   In the centre of Wales you'll find ...

   a) ☐ lots of farm animals.

   b) ☐ mountains that are higher than those in the US.

   c) ☐ the larger towns of Wales.

7   Most of the castles in Wales ...

   a) ☐ were built by a Welsh king to protect Wales from the English.

   b) ☐ were built by an English king to help him rule the people of Wales.

   c) ☐ have been completely destroyed.

8   What are **two** links between Wales and Australia?

   a) _____

   b) _____

3. Leseverstehen

Good health in Australia?

This article is from a British fitness and health magazine.

Sport, health and Australia seem to go together like bread, butter and jam. Australians have long been stars in rugby, cricket, tennis and sailing; now football has joined the list, with Australia present at each World Cup tournament since 1974. Australia won 35 medals at the 2012 London Olympics, their lowest showing since 1992. And yet even this figure put them way ahead of Britain, Germany or the United States in terms of medals per head of population.

Open any travel brochure with flights to Australia and happy groups of athletic-looking young people will smile at you from its pages. Search Australia's TV channels and slim, healthy individuals will beam at you from the screen, and not only in the adverts. Reality TV shows like *Bondi Beach* and *Surf Patrol* feature the work of volunteer life-savers on Australia's beaches. These men and women, who risk their lives while saving others from drowning and deal with dangers that range from sharks in the sea to thieves on the beach, have one thing in common: they are slim, healthy and agile.

No wonder Australia is such a popular destination for emigrants from Europe. More Brits who head abroad for life in a different country make their way to Australia than to any other country – over 200,000 between 2010 and 2015. During this period Australia was three times more popular than the USA, the second most popular destination for British emigrants. And the emigrants' happy stories of sunshine, barbecues, surfing, snorkelling and beach volleyball contrast with our indoor existence back in the UK. The Australian sun, we think, encourages Australians to keep fit; our dismal weather gives us a good excuse for sitting at home, reaching for the comfort food and putting on weight.

And yet the reality is different. Australia is in fact experiencing an explosion in obesity rates. Between 2014 and 2015, two in every three Australians were considered medically overweight or obese (overweight is defined as having some excess body fat, while obese is defined as having so much excess body fat that it has a negative effect on health). Ten years before, only just over half of Australians fell under this category. In today's obesity rankings, Australia is ahead of France and Germany. And as excess weight is a risk factor for heart disease, Type 2 diabetes and some cancers, the worry is that the country will see a dramatic increase in these diseases. Or, at the very least, Australia will face a rising bill for the medication to treat the conditions.

The reasons for the problem are basically a diet rich in salt, sugar and fat, and a lack of exercise. While almost half of all Australians consume the amount of fruit recommended in the national guidelines, only seven percent meet the target for vegetables. And while just over half of all Australians take part in 150 minutes of moderate physical activity per week, as recommended (or 75 minutes of vigorous activity), just under half do not. This includes almost 15 percent who confess to doing no physical activity at all – and these figures exclude those over 64 years of age.

Australia is of course by no means alone with this problem. It is a feature of modern life in many countries, and not only the wealthiest, for developing nations account for more than half of the world's obese population. And no country anywhere in the world has yet found a way of reducing its obesity rates. However, the huge rise comes as a particularly nasty surprise in Australia because it contrasts so starkly with the self-image of fitness and health. In future, it will be more and more difficult for the makers of the holiday brochures and TV series to find the slim and healthy Australians for their holiday photos and TV series.

- *First read the text.*
- *Then do the tasks (1–11).*
- *For tasks 1, 5, 8 and 10 tick the correct box.*
- *For tasks 3, 4, 6, 9 and 11 decide if the statements are true or false and tick the correct box. Then finish these sentences. You can quote from the text.*
- *For tasks 2 and 7 fill in the information.*

---

1 At the London Olympics in 2012 Australia won …

   a) ☐ more medals than ever before.

   b) ☐ the most medals since 1992.

   c) ☐ the fewest medals since 1992.

2 Australia won more medals than Britain, Germany or the United States if you consider …

_____

3 The life-savers shown on TV shows like *Bondi Beach* and *Surf Patrol* earn a lot of money.

   This statement is … ☐ true ☐ false … because the text says …

_____

4 One of the tasks of the life-savers is to prevent stealing.

   This statement is … ☐ true ☐ false … because the text says …

_____

5 When emigrants to Australia contact their families in Britain they …

   a) ☐ say that they sit at home and put on weight.

   b) ☐ give a positive picture of Australia.

   c) ☐ say that they lie on the beach all day.

6 About a third of all Australians weigh more than doctors recommend.

   This statement is … ☐ true ☐ false … because the text says …

_____

7 A growing number of Australians are medically overweight.

   Give **two** negative consequences, according to the text.

   a) _____

   b) _____

8 According to the figures in the text, one of the problems is that …

    a) ☐ hardly any Australians do the recommended amount of exercise per week.

    b) ☐ Australians eat too much meat.

    c) ☐ only a small minority of Australians eat enough vegetables.

9 These statistics don't include older Australians.

    This statement is …   ☐ true   ☐ false   … because the text says …

---

10 The rates of obesity …

    a) ☐ are worse in Australia than in any other country.

    b) ☐ have not gone down anywhere in the world.

    c) ☐ are only a problem of the richer countries in the world.

11 The image projected by the brochures and TV series is false.

    This statement is …   ☐ true   ☐ false   … because the text says …

Zweiter Prüfungsteil: Wortschatz – Schreiben

4. Wortschatz

Life in the Outback

Noah's parents are farmers in the Australian Outback. He describes life in the Outback for an online magazine.

> • *Fill in suitable words or tick the correct box.*

1   Most Australians live in large cities on the coast, like Sydney, for example, a city with a

   _____ of 5.25 million inhabitants.

2   Their lifestyle is in many ways ...
   a) ☐ likely   **b)** ☐ contrasted   **c)** ☐ comparable   **d)** ☐ reasonable
   with that of people living in any large cities anywhere in the world.

3   They battle through the morning rush hour to get to work, spend the day working in a multi-storey

   air-conditioned office _____, and struggle through the traffic to return

   home in the evening.

4   Life is very different for the minority of Australians who live in the Outback. There are no traffic

   jams here. In fact there often aren't _____ roads. Most people drive the

   last few miles home on earth tracks.

5   During the rainy season many of these are ...
   a) ☐ impassable   **b)** ☐ improbable   **c)** ☐ unprejudiced   **d)** ☐ impressed
   because they are so muddy.

6 The consequence is that people have to buy everything they need well in ...

a) ☐ account **b)** ☐ advice **c)** ☐ approach **d)** ☐ advance

and store things in huge stores and refrigerators.

7 In the dry season, on the other _____, there is often no rain at all for weeks.

8 In these times of drought there is an acute lack of water, and farmers in the Outback have to work extra hard to feed and water their sheep and ...

a) ☐ fields. **b)** ☐ cattle. **c)** ☐ flowers. **d)** ☐ beef.

9 Farmers often live miles away from their nearest neighbours, so they have to be clever and tough. In particular, they need to be able to survive and solve _____ on their own.

10 Primary and secondary schools can be far away, so the biggest problem for children in the Outback is their ...

a) ☐ employment. **b)** ☐ care. **c)** ☐ growth. **d)** ☐ education.

11 Children do lots of their lessons online, rather than in classrooms. The result is that they work and play alone. And they often feel lonely because they have so _____ contact with other children.

12 That's why barbecues and festivals are such an important feature of life in the Outback. People look _____ to them for months beforehand.

13 They are a chance for people to meet old friends and make new ones, a place where many ...

a) ☐ recommendations **b)** ☐ relationships **c)** ☐ repairs **d)** ☐ responsibilities

between young men and women begin.

5. Schreiben

Morwenna, a girl from Wales, has written an article for *Stand Up!*, an online magazine that posts unpopular or unfashionable opinions.

OK, I know it isn't cool to write positively about strict parents. Most people expect parents to smile at their children whatever they're doing. Parents are supposed to lead by example.
5 Endless books on parenting advise their readers to praise their children and give them positive messages, and warn them against being too strict.

This message is reinforced in TV series. If
10 we see a mother or father who insists that their child returns home by a certain time, or who tells them off for not tidying their room, we get the message that the parents are quick to anger or even aggressive.

15 But I want to challenge this view. You see, my parents have always been strict. In our house, there were rules, and my brother and sister and I soon learned to obey them.
20 When we were small, we had to wash our hands. We had to eat everything that was put on our plate – unless we had an allergy, of course. If we asked for something at the table and didn't say *Please*, we didn't get it. There was no second
25 chance. And we had electric toothbrushes that checked that we brushed our teeth for a full two minutes.

Does that sound as if my parents were too
30 strict? Well, I agree that there were times when I thought so too. My parents wanted to know the name of any film we wanted to watch – and they decided whether we would be allowed to watch it or not. I remember when I was invited
35 to a birthday party and the ten-year-old birthday boy wanted to watch the first *Harry Potter* film. Six of my friends were allowed to go and see the film; I was allowed to go and give a present and eat a slice of birthday cake, but I had to come
40 home before the others watched the film.

Now that I'm sixteen, I'm allowed to go to town and to the shops, but I have to message my mum or dad every hour so that they know I'm safe. And I always tell them where I'm going
45 and who with. In the evenings, I have to be home by nine o'clock – unless I'm going to the theatre.

Films are usually shown earlier in the day, but plays usually begin at 7.30 and finish after 9 pm, so I can't do anything about it.

It may all sound rather exaggerated or even a
50 bit frightening, but my point is that my parents love me very much, and I honestly believe that most of their rules have helped me in life. I take my personal hygiene seriously and have never needed treatment at the dentist. I have learned
55 to eat (and enjoy) all sorts of different foods. I don't think I was harmed because I watched *Harry Potter* at the age of 13 instead of ten. And I know that my parents take my safety very seriously. OK, it would
60 sometimes be nice to stay out longer than 9 pm – but on the other hand, because we're all home by nine, we sit together, chat about our day and have a real family life.
65 That's valuable too.

Of course there were times when I was jealous of my friends who could watch whatever film they wanted, who could say *No* to spinach and mushrooms,
70 and who didn't have to contact their parents when we were in town together. But I watch them now, and I see, for example, that many of them find it hard to keep their rooms tidy because they never had to do it when they were
75 small. I'm much more independent in that respect. I also notice that my friends fight with their parents much more than I do. They have endless discussions about rules, whereas in my family the rules have always been clear and we
80 live in harmony most of the time. This is important in a family of five.

I know that parents can be *too* strict. And I certainly don't agree with physical violence – my parents never ever yelled at me or hit me.
85 But all in all I feel that being too strict is maybe less dangerous than not being strict enough. It's hard when you're a child, but you understand the reasons when you're a bit older.

1 *Describe* what you know about Morwenna's home life.

2 *Explain* why Morwenna feels her parents' rules have been good for her.

3 You have a choice here. Choose **one** of the following tasks.

a) *"Friends teach you more about life than parents or teachers."*

Comment on the statement from your point of view.

Include the following aspects:
- *Give reasons for and against this statement.*
- *Give examples of situations that support your arguments.*
- *Write a conclusion and state how teenagers learn best about life.*

or

b) *Write a letter to the editor at* **Stand Up!** *to comment on Morwenna's article.*

Include the following aspects:
- *Say if you basically agree or disagree with Morwenna.*
- *Mention some aspects of her article and discuss these.*
- *Give examples of situations that support your arguments.*
- *Write a conclusion and state what rules are important for teenagers.*

Tipps für die Prüfung

Prüfungsvorbereitung

- **Beginne rechtzeitig mit dem Lernen und mache dir einen Lernplan**, bei dem du auch Wiederholungsphasen einplanst. Starte mit Aufgaben, die dir im Unterricht noch schwerfallen. Hake ab, was du bereits erledigt hast.

- **Überlege dir, wo du im Englischen noch grundsätzliche Probleme oder Lücken hast** (z. B. Grammatikprobleme, die immer wieder auftreten). Diese Themen kannst du dann mit den interaktiven Übungen auf www.scook.de gezielt noch einmal wiederholen.

- **Mache dich mit dem Ablauf der Prüfung und mit allen Aufgabenformaten vertraut**. Plane im Vorfeld, wie viel Zeit du für jeden Prüfungsteil und für die Kontrolle zur Verfügung hast.

- **Schreibe dir auf, wann und wo die Prüfung stattfindet**, und plane etwas mehr Zeit für den Weg ein als sonst.

- **Lege alle Materialien am Vorabend der Prüfung bereit** (z. B. funktionstüchtige Stifte, Uhr; Smartphones sind in der Regel nicht erlaubt!).

- **Achte auf ausreichend Schlaf und ein gutes Frühstück.**

Wenn du dich gut vorbereitet hast, kannst du selbstbewusst in die Prüfung gehen!

Während der Prüfung

- **Behalte die Zeit im Blick!** Am besten legst du während der Prüfung eine Uhr auf den Tisch und schaust von Zeit zu Zeit darauf. Wenn du an einer Aufgabe festhängst, gehe lieber erstmal zur nächsten Frage weiter. Nimm dir am Ende einige Minuten Zeit, um deine Antworten noch einmal durchzugehen.

- **Lies die Aufgabenstellung gründlich durch**, bevor du mit der Bearbeitung beginnst. Manchmal enthält eine Aufgabe mehrere Teilaspekte. Markiere sie und übersetze sie dir zur Sicherheit in deine Muttersprache.

- **Nutze deine Chance!** Auch wenn du unsicher bist, ob die Lösung stimmt, so ist es ratsam, die Aufgabe trotzdem zu bearbeiten. So hast du zumindest eine Chance, dass es richtig ist. Kreuzt du keine Lösung an oder lässt die Lücke leer, so bekommst du auf jeden Fall null Punkte.

- **Mache dir bei Schreibaufgaben Notizen, wenn du gut in der Zeit liegst.** Sie können dir helfen, deine Gedanken zu ordnen und deinen Text sinnvoll zu strukturieren. Beachte aber, dass nur dein endgültiger Text in die Bewertung eingeht.

- **Gib deinen Texten eine gute Struktur mit Einleitung, Hauptteil und Schluss.** Beginne jeden neuen Textteil mit einem neuen Absatz.

- **Formuliere klare Sätze.** Vermeide es, komplizierte deutsche Sätze wortwörtlich ins Englische zu übersetzen. Formuliere möglichst mit deinen eigenen Worten, es sei denn, die Aufgabenstellung verlangt ein Zitat aus dem Text (z. B. „Quote from the text.", „Give examples from the text.").

- **Kontrolliere am Ende**, was du geschrieben hast. Achte besonders auf Vollständigkeit, die Rechtschreibung, die Zeitformen deiner Verben und den Satzbau.

Wir wünschen dir viel Erfolg für deine Prüfung!

Übersicht über die Aufgaben zum Hörverstehen

Die Tonaufnahmen (MP3-Dateien) und die Hörtexte findest du online unter www.scook.de.
Deinen persönlichen Zugangscode findest du auf Seite 1 deines Abschlussprüfungstrainers.

Track	Kapitel	Titel	Seite
1	Training Section	Calgary's skyways (Part 1)	8
2	Training Section	Calgary's skyways (Part 2)	9
3	Training Section	Calgary's skyways (Part 3)	9
4	Training Section	Calgary's skyways (Part 4)	10
5	Training Section	Calgary's skyways (Part 5)	10
6	Training Section	The Niagara Falls (Version 1)	10
7	Training Section	The Niagara Falls (Version 2)	12
8	Training Section	The *Tour de Yorkshire*	13
9	Training Section	Bob Marley	14
10	Musterprüfung 1	Bo-Kaap – a special district in Cape Town	38
11	Musterprüfung 1	A presentation about William Shakespeare	39
12	Musterprüfung 2	A True Short Story	48
13	Musterprüfung 2	Cricket in India	49
14	Musterprüfung 3	The *D of E* expedition	58
15	Musterprüfung 3	A presentation about Wales	59
16	Urheberrechtserklärung		

Studio: Clarity Studio Berlin

Regie und Aufnahmeleitung: Christian Schmitz

Tontechnik: Christian Marx, Pascal Thinius

Illustrationen
Karen Donnelly, Brighton, UK (S. 9; S. 19; S. 21; Lösungsbeileger S. 2)